D1213288

Life Styles of Educated Women

Life Styles of Educated Women

ELI GINZBERG

WITH IVAR E. BERG, CAROL A. BROWN,
JOHN L. HERMA, ALICE M. YOHALEM,
AND SHERRY GORELICK

COLUMBIA UNIVERSITY PRESS
New York and London 1966

Library of Congress Catalog Card Number: 66-18060
Printed in the United States of America

IN MEMORY OF

Adele Oppenheimer and Harry George Friedman

and Francis Lee Friedman

THINE OWN FRIEND,

AND THY FATHER'S FRIEND

Preface

In the early 1960s, the Rockefeller Brothers Fund learned that the Conservation of Human Resources Project at Columbia University was conducting a study of talented persons under a grant from the Carnegie Corporation. The results of this study of intellectually able and talented men were published by the Columbia University Press in 1964 in a book entitled *Talent and Performance.* The Rockefeller Brothers Fund made it possible for us to expand our materials dealing with women, and later made an additional grant to enable us to broaden and deepen the scope of the study. This book and a second one, entitled *Educated American Women: Self Portraits,* which will appear in the fall of 1966, are the results.

In undertaking a study of a group of people the investigators are always confronted with two challenges: to identify the people to be studied and make contact with them, and to secure their cooperation. With respect to the first, the Conservation staff was particularly fortunate because of the wholehearted cooperation of the Columbia officials. Grateful acknowledgement is made of the help received from the following: Charles P. Hurd and Ralph Ellis, Office of the Registrar; Mark L. Piesch, director, and William D. Quesenbery, Jr., of University Admissions;

Athena Peters, University Placement; James F. Trosch, Central Records.

The several professional schools and graduate departments and individuals within them courteously and graciously aided our research: Teachers College, Robert A. Streeter; College of Physicians and Surgeons, Dr. George A. Perera; Public Health, Louise Gerold; Law, Frank K. Walwer; Journalism, Eileen Walsh; Library Service, Lucy M. Crissey; Social Work, Eleanor A. Moore.

Specific note should be taken of the 311 women who responded to our request for assistance. The questionnaire which we sent to them, and which is reproduced in the Appendix, could not be answered in less than several hours. Many respondents spent much more time in reviewing their experiences and committing them to paper. Moreover, each gave us permission to use all of her answers, subject only to our assurance that her anonymity would be preserved. Without the full participation of these women, their frank and open self-appraisals, this study would have been stillborn. We are in their debt.

In addition to those listed on the title page, the following participated as staff members at one stage or another: Lois Lipper, Ann Langenberg Riday, Arlene Shafran.

The many drafts of the manuscript were typed by Brenda Richmond, Paula Frank, Carol Fortin, Virginia Stevens Lieberfreund, and Sylvia Leef. Patrice LaLiberte of the University Publications Office advised on the printing of the questionnaire.

The manuscript was read by Dr. Douglas Bray, Director of Personnel Research, American Telephone and Telegraph Company, who gave us the benefit of his comments.

Ruth Szold Ginzberg advised us about the styling of the statistical tables and edited the manuscript.

ELI GINZBERG, DIRECTOR
CONSERVATION OF HUMAN RESOURCES

Columbia University
January, 1966

Contents

1. New Horizons 1
2. Our Group 15
3. Development and Education 28
4. Options and Decisions 47
5. Family and Community 59
6. Work and Careers 73
7. Occupational Achievement 95
8. Accommodation 108
9. Satisfactions and Fulfillment 130
10. Life Styles 144
11. Work in the Lives of Women 166
12. Policy 179

Appendix: Questionnaire Used in Life Styles Study 197
Bibliography 209
The Conservation of Human Resources Project 213
Index 217

I

New Horizons

In 1960, when the staff of the Conservation of Human Resources Project at Columbia University undertook a research investigation of the career development of a group of fellowship winners, its plans included a study of both men and women. Surely, we felt, discrimination on the basis of sex did not belong in a study of talent. The detailed questionnaire which we used in that study had been developed by members of the Conservation staff who happened to be male, and it had been pretested in a business environment in which the vast majority were men.

A scanning of the completed questionnaires showed us that something was awry. While some of the women filled in all of the requested information and returned the questionnaire without special comment, many others did not. Some said that the questionnaire did not fit their situation; some said they had not pursued a career. Others pointed out that the questions were much better suited to elicit information about the work and life experiences of men than of women. They mentioned, in particular, that the questionnaire gave them no opportunity to discuss their homes and families, or to trace the impact of these facets of their lives on the unfolding of their careers. Some respondents complained that the questionnaire provided no opportunity to report the many starts and stops that had characterized their work patterns. And still others stated that although men have careers, women have only jobs.

It soon became clear that, in our efforts to treat all fellowship winners alike, we had erred. The lives of these women, particularly the occupational aspects, had differed substantially from the patterns characteristic of the men. We, therefore, had to adjust our research plans. We decided to concentrate first on the men and, when our resources permitted, to undertake a special study of the women. The results of our analysis of the career development of men were published in 1964 under the title *Talent and Performance*. About a year earlier we had been able to focus attention specifically on women and to devise a questionnaire to take account both of the original criticisms and suggestions of our women respondents and of the lessons we had learned in carrying through the study of the men.

This book is based almost entirely on the information and evaluations thus elicited from a group of educated and talented women about the unfolding of their lives and careers. The staff has acted primarily as catalyst in organizing their replies. Our study therefore differs considerably from the vast bulk of literature that exists today about the changing role of women in modern society that has been contributed by philosophers, anthropologists, sociologists, historians, and other specialists, as well as by amateurs in a large number of popular writings on this theme.

The literature about the role of women can be distinguished by several different approaches. First are the moralists, whose analyses are directed to evaluating the key elements which operate to change the relation of the sexes in modern society. Most of these writers are strongly in favor of the trends which they see unfolding, such as the heavier involvement of married women in the world of work. Others are concerned that, because of their greater participation in the labor force, women are neglecting their primary duty to nurture the oncoming generation. Other writers, such as Betty Friedan, are equally convinced that in recent years the United States has tended to accentuate a pseudo-femininity which has had the result of stultifying the lives and wasting the talents of a great number of women. The Spring 1964 issue of *Daedalus*, subtitled "The Woman in America," provides an excellent collection of different views from a group of select and sophisticated contributors.

Less prolific but still noteworthy are the empiricists, who (though not directly concerned about the value implications of changes that are under way) have directed their efforts to describing and evaluating historical and statistical evidence. Among the most conspicuous examples of this approach was the study published in 1957 by the National Manpower Council entitled *Womanpower*. An insightful European effort to deal with parallel materials is the book by Alva Myrdal and Viola Klein, *Woman's Two Roles: Home and Work*, published in 1956.

Other analysts are concerned with women's education and careers: *Graduate Education for Women: The Radcliffe Ph.D.*, a report by a Faculty Trustee Committee (1956); *The American College*, edited by Nevitt Sanford (1961); and *The Academic Woman*, by Jessie Bernard

(1964), provide significant information that bears on the career development of particular groups of educated women.

Reference must be made to another group of investigators—those who, in the pursuit of specialized research in their several disciplines, have illuminated one or another facet of the occupational and life plans and experiences of large or small groups of women. Among the most interesting studies are those which have been directed to such questions as whether, and to what extent, differences in aptitude and interests between males and females are biologically or culturally determined, the parallels and differences in the educational and occupational planning of men and women, and the different role that work plays in their lives.

But with few (if any) exceptions, neither the moralizers, the empiricists, nor the discipline specialists have carried through a systematic investigation of the unfolding of the life experiences of a group of women with particular focus on their preparation for and involvement in the world of work.

Since we had learned from our earlier experience that it would be impossible to explore effectively the career development of a group of educated women by focusing narrowly on their preparation for work and their experiences at work, our revised plans provided for a much enlarged framework that would enable us to assess the interrelations among their roles as homemakers, workers, and members of the community. One of the striking differences that we found between our parallel investigations of the career development of men and of women was that the men followed a relatively simple and straightforward pattern compared with the much more complex career and life patterns characteristic of the majority of our women. In studying the men it was possible to place their career problems onto the center of the stage and to focus on these; it was necessary to pay only incidental attention to their lives off the job—as husbands and fathers and as members of communal organizations. Not so with the women. Each decision with respect to their jobs might have an even greater impact on their families than on their careers, just as actions with respect to their homes and children might have primary consequences in the job arena.

Time and again we were impressed by the fact that the men's study was infinitely less complicated than the women's. The difference between the two was sharply revealed when it came to a first draft of the results. We were able to organize and write up the results of the men's study in a straightforward fashion, to delineate the different facets of their occupational life within the framework of a few simple patterns. But in putting together the women's study, we encountered major difficulties. Each aspect with which we were concerned seemed to interact with many other facets; no one feature of these women's lives could be readily isolated for analysis.

This phenomenon has been observed by many other students and it has led most of them to center their analyses around the problems that modern women face. While we certainly would not deny, on the basis of our study, that most women are confronted with multiple problems, as are most men, we do not believe that this is the differentiating characteristic. Beyond their problems or, as some writers prefer to call them, their conflicts, these women face an even larger number of significant *options*. The term *prob-*

lem has a constricting and negative quality. The poor, the sick, the aged are beset by problems. But the pattern of these women's lives, while certainly not free of limitations and constraints, reflected in the first instance their responses to the wide range of choices which they had faced.

Some of the factors, primarily social, which have increased their options are not new; others reflect recent changes. Together they have created an increasingly more supportive environment for these women in which to choose a pattern of life and to follow it.

Among the long-term factors which have operated to broaden their choices, several stand out. There is a tendency, especially among those like ourselves who are concerned with the analysis and evaluation of contemporary materials, to exaggerate recent changes and to see a larger gap between the present and the past than more careful historical appraisal would justify. We will set forth briefly our understanding of the extent to which the patterns of women at work show evidence of continuity or change. We were fortunate in being able to make use of the investigations of one of our former staff members, Robert W. Smuts, who wrote an incisive volume on *Women and Work in America* (1959).

Schematically, we can say that in earlier centuries most women in America worked and they worked throughout the whole of their adult lives. In fact, whether a farm family was affluent or impoverished frequently hinged on the competence of the wife. The principal exceptions were the small minority of families in middle- and upper-income classes who lived in urban centers. The major change in the pattern of women's lives occurred after the Civil War when accelerating industrialization and urbanization ushered in a rapid increase in the urban middle class. More and more city women grew up without experience in the world of work, particularly after they married and started their families.

This isolation of women from work was a significant phenomenon in American life for only about eighty years —from the Civil War to World War II. And even during this period, women from lower income groups continued to work. Moreover, in the closing decades of the last century, and with increasing momentum in the first three decades of this century, a small but increasing number of women from the middle and upper classes entered the labor market; some pursued careers with intensity throughout their lives. Thus it is fatuous to read recent history as a reversal of a hallowed tradition in which women, particularly married women, kept away from the world of work. Such a pattern was established, but it was not a tradition, and surely not a hallowed one.

The next long-term trend relates to the American tradition of encouraging the education of women. For a great many decades more girls than boys graduated from high school, and although there have always been more men than women in college, women have long accounted for a substantial minority—roughly 2 out of 5. At the graduate level, the disparity between the sexes has been considerably greater: more men than women acquire a master's degree and many more earn a doctor's degree. But universities and professional schools have been open to women for decades and many women have taken advantage of the opportunity to pursue postgraduate education.

The relatively high family income in this country, and

the opportunities that students have to earn at least part of their expenses, have also facilitated the access of many women to higher education. Added to these favorable circumstances is the liberal support by state and a few local governments of college and university education.

The social emancipation of women in this country, together with the willingness of colleges to assume some responsibility for supervising their women students, has also added to the number who could obtain their parents' permission to go to college. In fact many parents skimped and saved in order to send a daughter to college, not only so that she could acquire more education and prepare for a job, but also, and very importantly, so that she might meet and marry an educated young man with a bright future.

We must note, however, that the vast expansion of secondary and higher education in this country started after the end of the Civil War, during a period when more and more married women did not work. This means that collegiate and higher education for women was fashioned during the few generations when only a handful of female students had career objectives and when even fewer women graduates pursued occupational goals after they married.

Nevertheless, while most parents expected that their daughters would eventually marry and therefore would not work, they recognized that a daughter who acquired a useful skill, such as teaching, could support herself in a genteel manner while she searched for a husband. Further, if perchance she did not marry or if her marriage foundered or her husband became ill or died, she would be in a position to take care of herself and her children. College education has always had this much of an occupational aspect for most women.

We have noted that in recent decades, more and more young women complete high school and go on to college. This fact has had a subtle impact on the attitudes and behavior of many of these women toward work. Many have become deeply interested in certain fields. Others became critical of the social mores which cut off middle-class married women from the opportunity to work outside of the home. Some so enjoyed the experience of working that they went to considerable lengths to continue to work after they married and had children. In short, higher education for women itself operated to alter the pattern which excluded married women from work.

Here are a few figures about the increase in the number of women who have completed higher education. At the turn of the century, women accounted for approximately 20 percent of all who acquired a baccalaureate or first professional degree. Three decades later they had considerably narrowed the gap between them and men. In 1930 women acquired 40 percent of all the baccalaureate degrees awarded. During these same three decades the proportion of the master's degrees which they received also doubled, again from about 20 to 40 percent. Only in the case of the doctorate did they continue to lag far behind; in 1930 they received roughly 15 percent of those awarded.

Because of the long depression of the 1930s and the erratic trends in higher education during and after World War II we will skip to 1960 as the next date for comparison. We find that women received 40 percent of all baccalaureate degrees awarded; they slipped back from 40 to 30 percent at the master's level; and their proportion of doctor's degrees slipped from 15 to 10 percent. These figures of course reflect their position relative to that of men. They hide the fact that the actual number of women completing higher education increased rapidly. In 1930 about 55,000 women received a bachelor's degree; the comparable figure for 1960 was 139,000; at the master's level the number increased from just below 6,000 to 24,000, and at the doctor's level from about 350 to 1,030.

These absolute and relative gains in the level of higher education achieved by women since the turn of the century can now be considered in relation to employment. In 1962 nearly three-fifths of all college-educated women were in the labor force, in contrast to two-fifths with high school diplomas and one-third who had not gone beyond grammar school. While these gross ratios mask other factors such as age and family income, they do suggest that the more education a woman has had, the more likely she is to be in the labor force.

To these long-term trends we can now add several recent factors which have helped to broaden the options of educated women in the shaping of their lives. During the first three decades of this century, there was a slow, steady rise in the proportion of married women in the labor force who worked out of preference rather than necessity. But the real breakthrough in employment for women came in World War II. The nation's leaders called upon the married women of the country to come out of their homes and go to work to further the war effort. A very large number responded. The barrier against married women in the middle- and upper-income classes was eliminated dramatically.

The women in our study belong to the first generation which was able to take advantage of this basic change in social mores from the start of their adult lives. If they decided to opt for both marriage and a career, they no longer were flying in the face of convention. The transformation wrought by the war was speedy and far-reaching. Thereafter, although discrimination against women continued to be more or less widespread in many sectors of the economy, fewer and fewer employers maintained that the *only* place for a married woman was in the home.

A second condition operating to broaden the options of educated women in the two decades since the end of World War II was the change in the labor market following the early breakthrough. These years witnessed marked increases in the demand for professional and other types of white collar workers; they saw the rapid growth of certain fields, such as teaching and nursing in which women had long been represented; and they saw reduced competition because of a decline in the number of new male workers as a result of the lowered birthrates of the Depression. In all of these regards, the late 1940s, 1950s, and the first half of the 1960s have been favorable to women who want to work.

The third of the newer factors that have contributed to a broadening of the options of educated women to shape their lives according to their preferences relates to home and family. Women have substantial control over the size of their families and they can run their homes with less time and energy than heretofore. Continuing wide diffusion of knowledge about contraception among the educated population carries a widened set of options for women including the possibility of sexual relations without marriage, deliberate postponement of childbearing, and limitation of the number of their children. At the same time, American industry was engaged in a continuing search for improved ways of helping women to simplify their housekeeping with the result that it was possible for a woman to spend less and less time on family chores. This had the further effect of decreasing the challenge that women found in housekeeping.

We have called attention to important changes in the economic and social environment which were operating to increase the number and proportion of married women who work—changes in the labor market, social mores, and patterns of homemaking. We have also seen that the extent to which young women are educated, particularly the larger numbers and proportions who attend and graduate from college and graduate school, apparently exercises an important influence on their attitudes and behavior with respect to work. This trend helps to explain the focus of the present investigation on educated women. Our group is a distinct minority but it is also the pace-setter. We confront a highly dynamic situation. The environment to which women must adapt is undergoing rapid change and, in turn, the way in which they are being brought up and educated to cope with this changing environment is undergoing rapid change.

In such a fluid situation there is no obvious or fixed point for a study of development. However, we believe that the broadened options for educated women are an important new fulcrum; they are therefore a major point of departure for our analysis.

More and more women have the opportunity to pursue higher education and we know that more and more of them are in fact exercising this option.

More and more married women are working. At the turn of this century the proportion in the labor force was approximately 1 in 6; today it is about 1 in 3.

More and more women with children under six are finding it practical to combine work and home. The proportion in 1940 was about 10 percent; in 1960 the proportion was about twice as large.

At the turn of the century about 1 in 7 women did not marry; it is possible that among those now reaching marriageable age the proportion who do not marry may be cut in half because of changes in personal freedom, family structure, and the world of work. Here is further evidence of broadened options. And the increase in divorce must also be recognized as an additional option.

These changes in education, the economy, and social mores are crucial, but they are not the only ones that have provided increased scope for the way in which women shape their lives. In addition to gains in personal and family income, potent factors such as improvements in the health of the population and in medical care have gone far to ease the burden of rearing children and have helped to alleviate the disturbances previously associated with the menopause. Another factor is the expansion of opportunities for less than full-time work.

There are, of course, forces pulling in the opposite direction which tend to restrict rather than to enlarge the options of women. Three in particular should be noted: the rising standards of child rearing with its great stress on mother-child relationships; the difficulties which middle-class families face in attracting and keeping competent domestic help; and the relocation of younger middle-class families from the central cities to the suburbs which introduces a formidable transportation hurdle for many women who want to work.

We will begin our analysis by setting forth the characteristics of the women in our group and of the homes in which they grew up and we will review their educational experiences. In the chapters which follow we will then outline the options which these women faced and the decisions which they made with regard to the important areas of family and work.

We will then review the types of accommodations which they made to realize their objectives more effectively and we will assess the extent to which they are satisfied with their efforts and accomplishments. We will then seek to differentiate these women in terms of four basic styles which characterize the different patterns of their lives.

The penultimate chapter represents an effort to contribute to a more general theory of the role of work in the lives of women. The final chapter sets forth our recommendations for the more effective development and utilization of the potentials and skills of women.

This is the structure of the book. We are not committed to any position. We do not have a set of opinions about what is right and what is wrong. We have analyzed as objectively as possible the rich materials which a group of educated women placed at our disposal about the way in which they shaped their lives.

2

Our Group

To study any group, investigators must either depend on information which already exists or obtain new information. We became involved in the second type of investigation which required, first, the identification of a significant group and, second, its willingness to cooperate in furnishing the facts.

We sought a group who would meet three criteria—pursuit of education beyond college, demonstration of a high order of intellectual ability, and membership in a generation with markedly broadened options—and we found it among the women who had attended Columbia University in the immediate postwar years. We selected Columbia because of the assistance we could anticipate receiving from the authorities in identifying and making contact with these women, the wide range of graduate departments and professional schools from which we could select our group, and the high academic standards which would permit us to accept the judgments of teachers that certain women had intellectual ability.

It might be asked why we limited ourselves to a single institution instead of developing a representative sample from a large number of institutions. The answer is simple. Ours was an exploratory investigation aimed at uncovering the process of decision-making followed by a group of educated women who confronted a wide range of opportunities and some constraints at successive periods of their adolescence and young adulthood. It was essential that we develop a framework before seeking to carry through a study of a representative sample. The Columbia group, representing a cohort of women who pursued graduate studies between 1945 and 1951, met our requirements.

Our desire to include only women with significant intellectual ability led us to limit the group to those who had won fellowships or scholarships, stood high in their class, or had been elected to societies whose membership was chosen from among the best students. Some of our group met two or more of these conditions.

The women were chosen from throughout the university, from each of the graduate faculties as well as from the professional schools, excepting only engineering and dentistry. Each had at least one year of graduate study. While most of them acquired at least one graduate degree, this was not a basis of selection since we were interested in learning also about women who could not complete their work for a degree.

As we have indicated, our first approach was part of a study of both men and women. Since we eventually developed a substantially modified questionnaire for the study of the women, we sent a supplemental one to those women who had responded to the first one. Seventy-three filled in the supplemental questionnaire and are included in this study. In addition, 238 women answered the revised questionnaire, making a total of 311.

Approximately three out of four whom we succeeded in locating cooperated. The fact that such a high proportion responded is probably explained by the following. Most people like to talk about themselves. Some may have felt an obligation to cooperate with the university. Still others may have been worn down by our repeated follow-up communications. The respondent who surmised that "few will answer the questionnaire and those who complete it are a highly selected group" was mistaken, as was another who remarked that the "sampling will be limited to particularly conscientious women—the more passive women will simply leave it on their desk and never get around to it."

From the records available at Columbia University and from information in various biographical compendia and in other sources we were able to make a rough comparison between those who did not reply and those who took the time and trouble to fill out the questionnaire. This comparison revealed that there are no striking differences between the two groups with regard to their fields of study, marital status, number of children, principal field of work, and work history.

In our earlier study of male fellowship winners we had used a structured questionnaire and we had learned that a carefully designed and integrated set of questions could elicit a wealth of objective information together with subjective reactions, reflections, and evaluations. In light of this successful experience, we saw no reason to change this approach for the present study. We were not concerned with probing the whole matrix of motivational forces that underlies the behavior of any particular individual. Nor were we interested in merely collecting statistical information. We wanted to elicit enough information so that we could determine the part that work had come to play in the lives of these women and to understand the major forces that were operating to bring about the patterns which we were able to discern. Some respondents were unhappy about our approach since we did not make our objectives and methods too explicit. When returning her completed questionnaire, one commented: "I must say I think statistical generalities are for the birds and I can't see how you can expect to arrive at any real conclusion from answers to questions like these. . . . They completely disregard the uniqueness of every individual which is the most important aspect."

The individual is the most important element in many studies—but not in the present investigation. We were not concerned with exploring the psychological connections between a woman's unconscious attitudes toward her femininity and her career orientation. Such explorations would require other instruments capable of probing into the psychological realms. Our primary concern was with delineating the changing role of work in the lives of these women against the background of their major interests and commitments. We believed that these connections were ascertainable from information that could be secured through the use of a structured questionnaire. We believed that the linkages which we sought could be ferreted out and we had no reason to expect that our respondents would falsify the information. The questionnaire approach left some, but by no means all, of our respondents uneasy. One wrote: "I don't know exactly what points you are trying to clarify or illustrate. I find this questionnaire frustrating. I would prefer a depth interview conducted by a skillful interviewer."

Others had a positive response. "Because this questionnaire has forced me to do a great deal of self-analysis, it has clarified my own thinking. I feel as if I have just concluded a nondirective counseling session. . . . Frankly, my delay in answering has been [due to] the fact that the questionnaire is so long and interrelated that I could not do it piecemeal." Another wrote: "Obviously I am in the same exploratory stage as your survey which seemed amazingly well timed for me." Another apologized for the delay in responding, adding that the questionnaire "became a part of my life for the last few months and I just took a long time with it."

The questionnaire, which is reproduced in the Appendix, gave the respondents an opportunity to do more than reply briefly to thirty-nine questions. The last question asked the respondents to elaborate or clarify any of their answers or to comment on any other points that they considered important. To encourage them to write at length, three and a half blank pages were provided. It is worth noting that 229, or 74 percent of the entire group, were sufficiently interested and cooperative to respond to this suggestion and many not only used up all of the available space but attached additional pages. Although some doubted the validity of the instrument, most of the group had a positive response.

One final point: since we did not ask highly personal questions, we can assume that the replies which we received reflect the respondents' best judgment of the facts. In fact, many of the responses were very frank and tended to provide more information than we requested.

These then are the reasons for our selection of this group and for the methods used. There remains one other preliminary task—to summarize the characteristics of the group so that the reader will have some idea of its background, development, and present circumstances.

The type of education that young people receive and the kind of persons they marry is conditioned to a marked degree by the families from which they come and the opportunities which their families have been able to provide. This applies even more to girls than to boys who, because of their easier access to higher education and their stronger dedication to a career, have somewhat greater mobility. We will therefore begin this discussion of the major characteristics of our group by reporting briefly on the families from which our women came.

Both parents of 68 percent of our women had been born in the United States or Canada; one or both parents of 26 percent were immigrants. The remaining 6 percent of the women were themselves born abroad. Included in our group were 6 American Negroes and 6 Americans of Oriental descent.

As one would expect to find at a major university, the students came from every section of the country. However Columbia draws a disproportionate number from the Middle Atlantic states. Most of our women had been born and had grown up in the leading metropolitan centers—New York, Chicago, Los Angeles, Philadelphia, Detroit—in other large cities or in suburban communities. Only about 1 in 4 had grown up in a small town or on a farm. Most of these girls had spent their formative years in an environment where new trends affecting women, including the new pattern of married women working out of the home, were accepted.

Other factors also encouraged them to have a positive stance towards higher education. At least one parent of 60 percent of the women in the group was a college graduate. Nevertheless, the 40 percent who did not have such a model also became interested in higher education and succeeded in earning at least one degree.

Their fathers' work and income was a major part of the developmental experiences to which these girls were exposed, since these factors determined the families' standards of living and social positions. Just over one-third of the fathers held a professional, academic, or executive position, such as physician, dean, consulting engineer. Just under a third were in the same broad occupational band but held somewhat less important jobs. The remainder were those who held clerical or selling positions and those who were craftsmen or farmers.

In order to obtain a single construct to describe the circumstances under which they grew up, we developed a simple nine point index based on father's occupation, mother's education, and estimated average family income, weighted equally. The resulting distribution revealed that 33 percent of the families fall in the upper third of the scale, 44 percent in the middle, and 23 percent in the lower part.

On the basis of information for about four-fifths of the group, we find that most of the women had grown up in small families. About three-fifths had been only children or had only one sibling. Only one-fifth had three or more siblings.

While the questionnaire did not specifically ask for information about the religion of the respondents we were able to ascertain this for almost 90 percent of the entire group from answers they provided about their various affiliations and the activities in which they engaged. Almost two-thirds were Protestants, Jews accounted for one quarter, and Catholics for only 9 percent. The relatively high proportion of Jews reflected, in part, the location of Columbia in New York City, and the markedly low proportion of Catholics reflects the known fact that they have been slow to pursue graduate education and even slower to make use of secular institutions.

The educational background of these women can be characterized, first, by the type of institution from which they had received their baccalaureate degrees. A significant

TABLE 2.1

Type of Institution	*Percent*
One of the Seven Sister colleges *	18
Other women's college	16
Coeducational college	23
University	34
Teachers or other specialized college	6
Foreign (other than Canadian)	3
Total	*100*

* Barnard, Bryn Mawr, Mt. Holyoke, Radcliffe, Smith, Vassar, Wellesley.

proportion of the women in our group were graduates of academically strong colleges or universities and only very few pursued a specialized course of instruction during their undergraduate years.

One of our respondents took us to task for not exploring in more detail the question of secondary school preparation: "Very little has been asked about pre-college education. Yet the superb education and social poise I received as a student of——[a private girl's school] probably has had a greater influence on my life than college." Although we did not request information about their pre-college education, we know from their comments that most of the group had attended public high schools and that few would agree with this emphasis on the importance of pre-college education.

As we have indicated, one of the advantages of using a large university as the locus for the study is the diversity of fields of concentration which it offers. Our 311 women had pursued their graduate studies in eleven major divisions of the university. Approximately 2 out of 5 had pursued studies in the humanities, social sciences, or natural sciences; the remainder had enrolled in one of the following: education,

TABLE 2.2

Department	*Percent*
Humanities	17
Social Sciences	16
Natural Sciences	9
Medicine and law	7
Social Work and public health	22
Business and journalism	11
Education and library science	18
Total	*100*

social work, library science, journalism, business, law, medicine, and public health.

This percentage distribution is not representative of the total number of women graduate students at Columbia. Our aim was to include able female students from as many divisions of the university as possible and not to concentrate on one or a few departments.

At the time they replied to the questionnaire in June, 1963, their educational achievement was as follows: slightly more than 33 percent had earned a doctor's degree, either a Ph.D. or a professional doctorate; 9 percent had completed all of their work for the doctorate except for finishing their dissertations; 55 percent had obtained degrees beyond the baccalaureate level other than a doctorate; less than 2 percent had only a baccalaureate degree. Since these figures do not take into account the number of women with more than one advanced degree, or those who are currently enrolled in courses leading to an advanced degree, or those who have undertaken graduate studies without a degree objective, we see that the group was indeed composed of women with an extraordinary amount of education.

TABLE 2.3

Age	*Percent*
33–36	11
37–40	35
41–44	27
45–48	11
49–52	9
53 and over	7
Total	*100*

Since our women were in graduate school in the late 1940s, their median age in 1963 was about forty. Table 2.3 summarizes their age distribution. The 16 percent who were forty-nine years old or older were for the most part women, who after years of work, had started or returned to graduate work at the end of World War II. Most of the others had proceeded to graduate school with little interruption after graduating from college.

Another characteristic is their marital status: 60 percent were married and living with their husbands when they responded to the questionnaire. An additional 12 percent had been married but their marriages had ended by death or divorce; half of these had remarried. The remaining 28 percent were single. Only 1 in 5 of the single women was less than forty years old, which suggests that it is unlikely that many will marry in the future. The proportion of single women in our group is much greater than in the population as a whole.

Of the 223 women who are, or who had been, married, 18 percent have no children and 14 percent have one child. At the opposite extreme, about 12 percent have four or more children. The majority—56 percent—have two or three children. Since most of the women have passed their thirty-fifth birthday, it is reasonable to assume that most of them have completed their families.

A major determinant of the type of lives which these women were able to fashion was the kind of men they married. Forty percent of the husbands had a doctorate (either a Ph.D. or professional degree), and an additional 12 percent had completed all the work required for a doctorate except the dissertation. Only one-quarter did not have at least one graduate degree.

We have information about the present occupations of the husbands of 205 of our women. Of this group, 60 percent are at the top of the occupational hierarchy, in a preferred professional, academic, or executive position. Most of the remainder are also on a high occupational level but hold positions carrying less prestige, such as managers of small businesses. Less than 5 percent have jobs which are lower on the occupational scale, such as salesmen or clerical workers.

A further dimension of the positions held by their husbands is their income. Only about 1 out of 4 earns less than $10,000 annually and 1 in 5 earns in excess of $20,000. It is likely that most of these men are still some distance from their maximum earning power, but their current income is sufficient to enable their families to live adequately, although only a few live in luxury.

So much for the principal characteristics of our group. By way of summary, we can say that a high proportion of these young women grew up in families in which the conditions predisposed them to pursue higher education, surely through college and possibly beyond. The majority were children of native born parents who wanted to help their daughters attain a good position in American society.

The fact that such a high proportion of the girls had Protestant parents who were well established in the major urban complexes of the nation and who had restricted the number of their offspring gave these girls broad options.

Those who married were in a good position to pattern their lives according to their desires and values because of their own superior education and the educational background and economic position of their husbands; and those who remained single were in a good position, by virtue of their family background and education, to pursue their career goals.

Many observers have noted that American society resembles a moving escalator. A high proportion of each generation moves ahead of its parents at the same time that there is a general elevation in the standards of living of the society. And this seems to have been so in the instant case. These young women were on the average better educated than their mothers, and they married men who on the average had more education than their fathers and who stood somewhat higher than their fathers on the occupational and income ladder.

In relation to the story which is to be unfolded in the following chapters, the most important finding emerging from this preliminary sketch is the confirmation that many of these young women had a wide range of options while they were growing up and after they reached adulthood. Most of them were in a position to attend college and graduate school without undue hardship. It was largely up to them to determine whether they wanted to marry, when and whom, and whether they wanted a large or small family or none at all. While their husbands' incomes were modest in the early years of marriage, they soon reached levels which provided some discretion about alternative expenditures. They often could live in better houses and in better neighborhoods than their parents, depending in part on their other preferences and needs. Almost all were able to hire some help to lighten their housekeeping chores.

No individual, regardless of financial resources, has unlimited options. The way in which these women ordered their lives by seeking a balance between their aspirations and reality in the areas of education, work, and family is the main concern of this book.

3

Development and Education

The kind of adult that an individual becomes reflects, among other factors, the many influences and experiences to which he was exposed from the day of his birth until he reaches an age when he becomes responsible for himself. Therefore, any effort to study a group of adults requires that attention be focused on major forces that have had an impact on their goals and behavior, such as the influence of parents and other key persons, the attitudes and values which prevailed in their environment, and major external occurrences such as a war or depression.

For our study, we are interested particularly in those influences and experiences which helped to determine the amount and type of education and training which these young women undertook, their objectives and goals, and their recognition of their broadened options with respect to work, career, marriage, and children.

Any effort to condense the first twenty-five years of an individual's life must necessarily be highly selective. With our group, we have chosen to concentrate on their parents, their education, and their anticipations.

The influence that parents exercise on their children is a result of both actions and attitudes. A child's earliest and usually strongest model is the parent of his own sex. Therefore, we will review briefly the mothers of the women in our group. We will describe in outline what these mothers did with their time and energy and how their daughters responded to them as models.

Although, as we have pointed out, World War II marked a significant breakthrough in the participation of married women in the world of work, it is noteworthy that only 26 percent of the mothers of these girls had never held a job, either before or after their marriage. Three-quarters of these mothers had worked at some time.

While 31 percent of these mothers had worked only prior to their marriage, a somewhat larger proportion—41 percent—had also worked after their marriage. In fact, about 14 percent of the mothers had worked continuously while their daughters were growing up, and about the same percentage worked intermittently during this period. Thus about 30 percent of our young women had had a working mother. We can assume that many of these mothers gave some indication of their feelings about working.

We asked our respondents about the influence of their mothers' work experience on their own career decisions. Over 60 percent of the group reported that the employment status of their mothers had had no effect on their own career decisions, or at least that they were not aware of any influence; of the quarter of the group who recognized an effect on their own decisions, the largest number reported that their mothers had worked after their marriage. In fact, 2 out of every 3 girls whose mothers had worked after marriage reported that this had an effect on their own plans. Almost all saw the influence as positive: while they were growing up, they looked forward to emulating their mothers and combining home and work.

This is how some of the women in our group commented on the influence of their mothers' working on their own attitudes and values. "I accepted, as a matter of course, that I would work after marriage." "All the women in my family worked. It was expected that I would." A third said: "It may have provided a model of a woman who managed successful motherhood with satisfying and enriching part-time work." The most positive statement was that "undoubtedly my mother's employment during all of my years of memory affected my decision that family and outside career were susceptible of combination. It never occurred to me that they were not." Not all the respondents reacted positively to the model of a working mother: "I felt that I wanted to be home with my young children. When I was young, we had a sleep-in maid since my mother worked." However, such reactions were rare.

Those whose mothers did not work after marriage had relatively little to say about whether this influenced their own career plans, although a few sought to combine homemaking and a career because they wanted to avoid being like their mothers. A respondent who became a professor at a leading university and who has two children remarked: "My mother's lack of an occupation influenced me in the sense that it made me want one." Another respondent stated that she felt that her mother's "college degree was a waste of time since she devoted herself to doing dishes and dusting." She herself has worked continuously except for three maternity leaves. Another, the mother of two children, who has worked steadily, recalled that her mother's "restlessness in the house made me realize the limitations of domestic activity for a restless mind and early made me decide not to repeat her experience."

While the mother's role may be the most important single influence on the shaping of her daughter's life, fathers also exercise a significant influence. Since fathers carry the principal career role in most middle-class families, some of our women shaped their ideas about work and working on the basis of their fathers' pattern rather than their mothers'.

The education to which young people aspire as well as the level of their actual educational achievement is greatly affected by parental attitudes and assistance. We noted in the preceding chapter that at least one parent of 3 out of 5 of the women in our group was a college graduate. In general, most parents want their children to receive at least as much education as they have acquired and preferably more.

Another consideration is the connection which parents perceive between education and occupational goals. In the past, a considerably higher proportion of boys than girls attended college because parents believed that the costs involved were more justified for sons who had to prepare to earn a living, than for their daughters who were likely to marry and be supported by their husbands. As noted above, many parents who question the value of a college education for their daughters in terms of a career send them to college nevertheless on the ground that it is a sound investment, at least in terms of "husband-hunting."

In addition, many immigrant parents, realizing that education is an escape route from the alien past into the new society, set high educational goals for their children and push their daughters as well as their sons to go to college. This is how one daughter of immigrant parents recalled her youth: "My parents were immigrants with little education, but with great ambition and ideals . . . and instilled in their children a strong sense of ambition, responsibility, duty, and patriotism. . . . It worked on me . . . and on my siblings. My mother was the best damn American there ever was!"

Another determinant is the trend in educational preparation characteristic of the society at large and particularly of the socioeconomic group to which the individual and his family belong. Since the level of educational preparation for the nation as a whole has been steadily rising, parents in every socioeconomic level have tended to desire more and more education for their children.

These are some of the pressures in the society at large and within the family which have helped to propel women to college and beyond. Another factor is personal. The young woman may consider higher education to be an essential element in her own development. She may want to learn just for the sake of acquiring an education, without specific reference to any other end, occupational or marital. This drive toward self-development is important.

These three sets of determinants—parental, environmental, and personal—establish the individual's aspirations with regard to education and play a significant role in determining their achievement. Parents who believe in the importance of education will save and sacrifice so that their children can obtain it. A society which places a high value on education is likely to make opportunities available. And the individual who is determined to go to college or graduate school will usually find a way to do so.

The families in which these young women grew up generally created a favorable environment for their pursuit of high educational objectives. Of the 9 out of 10 who reported on their parents' attitudes, 84 percent said that their parents had encouraged them and another 6 percent said that their parents were neutral but supported any of their plans. Only 6 percent reported that both parents were opposed to their going to college and another 4 percent said that one parent was opposed.

These are examples of how the women in our group assessed the general atmosphere in their families toward their education and their future. "I can never recall their expressing any expectations other than that I should get as much education as I wanted, find interesting work, and have a happy marriage. I have met all but the last of these, which is a fair batting average." Another reported that she "was reared in a protected, indulgent, comfortable family by well-educated sensible parents. . . . They made it easy for me to continue my education as long as I wished, supplementing the scholarships and fellowships I was given with decent allowances." Much the same support is reflected in the following: "My parents were wealthy so I did not find that my extended education was an imposition."

Many respondents reported the positive attitudes of their parents: "They always encouraged me to get as much as I wished (even though they didn't always understand what I was doing)." Or again: "My parents were anxious that I have a college education and both worked toward that end. My father did not care especially about what I did with my education, other than that I have a satisfied and happy life."

Others reported that their parents actually objected to

their acquiring a college education. One respondent reported: "We fought one another every inch of the way; they believed in high-school education and a secretarial job for me, and marriage within my own social, economic, and religious circle. I ended up quite differently." Another wrote: "My father believed college and graduate school were wasted on girls because they simply wasted the investment when they married. I believe this attitude strengthened my own desire for an education even though I had to finance it myself by working as a secretary through college and garnering fellowships for graduate school." And another: "Dad considered the education of his sons more important, but I think that this merely stiffened my resolution." It is important to note in passing that our group included only those girls who had succeeded in overcoming their parents' opposition. Many others undoubtedly gave way.

How the parents of our group felt about their daughters' preparation for and pursuit of careers and parental attitudes toward combining work with marriage and children was also an important influence on these women's emerging values and plans. They may not have known how their daughters would be able to juggle or combine the two but most parents apparently did not discourage their daughters from venturing the attempt.

About 30 percent of our group did not report any clear-cut parental attitudes toward the career-marriage complex. For those who did report such attitudes, the findings are quite different from what we might have anticipated: 36 percent reported that their parents favored preparation for a career and remained silent on the question of marriage; 12 percent reported that their parents advised them to prepare for a career but to look forward to combining it with marriage; 25 percent described their parents as generally supportive, which meant that they would not challenge any reasonable goal that their daughters set for themselves; 27 percent indicated that their parents strongly preferred that they plan for marriage.

Even if the "silent" group believed, in accordance with the mores of our society, that the principal challenge facing their daughters was to make a suitable marriage, a substantial majority had a positive attitude toward their daughters' plans to work. Only a minority of parents believed, as some reported: "Their attitude was that women should marry and never work." "It was assumed as long as I can remember that I would go to college and marry. No thought was given to my preparing for a career." The following type of comment was more frequent: "Both parents felt that education was extremely important and a career essential which should be combined in time with marriage." "My parents believed in professional education and work for women who desire them—they always encouraged me to think in terms of combining marriage with interesting work." "They did feel that girls should have career education so that even though they married, if there was any need to work, they could hold well-paying positions."

A small number of respondents reported that their parents were explicitly concerned with their careers. One reported an entire family orientation toward work for women: "Not only did my mother work, but great-grandmothers, grandmothers, and aunts. All were self-employed and worked with their husbands unless they were widowed—then they carried on ranches and businesses, usually both. Family attitude seemed to be 'this is ours, let's work together.' My maternal great-grandfather authored the bill which founded——Women's University 'to teach women how to make a living, not just sip tea.' " Much the same attitude though less pronounced was described in the following report: "They encouraged all of us (boys and girls) to plan for college, and they also taught us that it was important for girls—as well as boys—to be able to do some useful work." Or again: "Father felt strongly that women should have a profession to enable them to be independent even after marriage."

The comments about parents' attitudes toward marriage were interesting. A college instructor who has remained single remarked: "They never encouraged me to marry, which is one reason I let it go till it was too late to do anything about it." Other attitudes were more subtle: "They expected me to marry (I didn't) and were apologetic about me on that score with their friends, but never approved of anyone I ever went with." Extreme pressure not to marry was reported by another respondent: "My mother was so strongly in favor of my 'career' that she almost committed suicide when I decided to marry. I still believe that she really meant this, although she didn't carry out her threat."

The pervasiveness of the influence of the family environment on the general development of these young women is further illuminated by the following comments. A social worker wrote: "I am sure that Dad's successful, complete absorption in business influenced me toward human-being interests which he neglected. Also the contrast of my parents' emotional distress and eventual divorce in the midst of financial comfort and plenty gave me some perspective on the limitations of money and the necessity of working for other values." A classics professor saw direct linkages between her home and later life: "Our Greek background and interest in ancient culture . . . trips to Greece as a child . . . all these led me directly to archeology." A physician speculated: "My mother's goal for my brother was medicine but he quit college after one year. I somehow, without awareness, took over this goal during my teens." A professor of zoology wrote: "I think my father's inability to get much work during the depression made me uncomfortable in the presence of others of my age group and led to my drive to find a way of life as independent of others as possible."

What we find is that the parents of our group generally held a strongly positive attitude toward their daughters' pursuit of higher education, and those who were able helped them realize their plans. Next, a significant proportion of parents encouraged their daughters to think seriously about preparing for a career and a much larger number supported their daughters if they reached such a decision on their own.

With regard to the parents' attitudes toward their daughters marrying, it is difficult to accept our data at face value since they suggest that only a relatively small minority of parents pressed their daughters to marry and to look forward to a life as wife and mother. That they did not *press* their daughters is clear. But we cannot conclude that most of them did not want their daughters to marry. A more likely explanation is that most of them assumed that their daughters would marry and did not need special encouragement. But even if this was the hope and expectation of most parents, it did not lead them to discourage their daughters from seriously pursuing their preparation for work.

These were the parental attitudes and influences to which our respondents were exposed. How did they respond to them? The answers can be found in the way they undertook their education. While society can make educational facilities available and parents can encourage their children to make constructive use of them, the final decision rests with the individual. Only individuals who really want to acquire knowledge for its own sake or for other ends, such as preparation for a career, are able and willing to make the necessary investment of effort and concentration.

The heavy concentration of college women in the humanities indicates that the majority do not relate their studies closely to career objectives. Some select a few courses in education in order to qualify, if the need or desire should arise, for teaching. However, only a minority of women are career oriented while in college.

In our group, very few attended a specialized college or pursued a course of studies such as nursing, teaching, or home economics, which leads directly to a career. Only a small minority followed programs that were clearly professional.

Whatever the initial reason for the selection of a college major may be—and there are of course considerations other than interest alone—the fact that an individual pursues one major and eschews another has significance for his later choices and options. At some time in college the student can no longer jump from one field to another without paying a price. And as he gets farther along, the price keeps mounting.

In this connection, let us review the major fields of study that these young women eventually chose in graduate or professional school and see how they are related to their college majors. Using certain equivalents, such as English in undergraduate school and journalism in graduate school, or biology in college and medicine in professional school, we see that 56 percent of our women pursued the same major in graduate school as in college. Another 28 percent shifted their concentration a little but remained within the same broad area—such as those who shifted from one social science to another or from one natural science to another. Only 16 percent of the group selected a field of graduate study that had no relationship to their undergraduate major. There was therefore a significant element of continuity in the choice of courses made by 5 out of 6 of these young women. There was, then, substantial stability in their interests.

How committed were they to the field of study which they pursued in graduate school? Half of the group said that they had never considered an alternative major. The other half, who at least had considered an alternative, gave reasons for staying with the field of study they had already chosen: 39 percent of this second half decided that on balance they enjoyed the field which they had originally chosen; an additional 11 percent were able to satisfy their other interests through supplemental courses; and 10 percent recognized unattractive aspects of work in a contemplated alternative field. In short, 3 out of 5 discarded an alternative which they had considered. The others, who would have preferred to shift because of a weakening or change of interest, stayed with their original choice because they were dissuaded by their teachers or were uncertain about their ability in a new field. These findings indicate that these young women were more or less "hooked" into their field of interest by the end of college and certainly after the beginning of their graduate studies.

We have stated that a high proportion of young women are propelled along the route of higher education by an interest in their studies and only secondarily by their career objectives. We are in a position to test this proposition by reviewing the reasons that these young women offered for undertaking graduate studies. We have information about this from all but 9 of the 311 women: 35 percent reported that they could prepare for their chosen career only through graduate studies; 22 percent who had had work experience stated that graduate studies would enable them to gain skill and advancement in their work. What of the other 43 percent? What were their motivations? About half indicated that they "enjoyed" their studies and had an interest in their field. But they said not a word about any career goal. Most of the others mentioned external influences that propelled them to further study, such as the influence of family, teachers, or the winning of a fellowship.

The stability of their educational and career goals while they were in college and graduate school was striking. Of the entire group, 31 percent had a single career goal to which their education was closely geared; 14 percent shifted to a related goal during the course of their studies. This makes a subgroup of 45 percent with marked stability in their career objectives. Another 23 percent did not have clearly defined occupational goals during the earlier period of their education but eventually developed sharply defined career objectives. These subgroups comprise 68 percent of the entire group. Thus, 2 out of every 3 of these women had clear career objectives, early or late, during the course of their undergraduate or graduate studies, and except for minor shifts, these career goals tended to remain stable.

What was the experience of the other third of the group? The largest subgroup shifted while at college or graduate school from one career goal to another that was quite unrelated. The next largest number had a career goal at one point of their college or postgraduate life, but ended their graduate studies very much at sixes and sevens: they had no clearly defined plans. The remainder, only a small number, never developed any career goals: their objectives were limited to getting a good education and to marrying.

These figures show that many of our women had well-crystallized career objectives at the start of their graduate studies and that many others clarified their objectives as they continued to study. Only a minority left graduate school without having affirmed an occupational choice.

A further indication of the directedness and purposefulness with which these women pursued their education and career goals comes from consideration of the ages at which they acquired their baccalaureate and advanced degrees. All but 10 percent of the entire group had graduated from college by the time they were twenty-four; 20 percent were no older than twenty. Just under half of the entire group had their first advanced degree by the time they were twenty-four. Slightly over one-third had continued their education without interruption and slightly under one-third had an interruption of from one to four years. The remaining third left college or university for periods ranging from five to twenty-one years.

Slightly over one-third of all the women in the group acquired a doctorate. Most of them earned this degree when they were in their thirties, and about a third had completed their doctoral studies by the time they were twenty-eight.

Apparently a high proportion of the group was concerned with accomplishing certain educational and career objectives prior to taking on the added responsibilities of home and children. At twenty-four and even at twenty-eight a smaller percentage was married than had acquired an advanced degree.

At least brief attention should be paid to other influences to which these young women were exposed during their adolescence and young adulthood which affected their decisions about the future. When asked about the influence of "key persons," the respondents singled out teachers in high school and even more, teachers in college. Peers played a minor role as did husbands and employers. For example, a professor of home economics wrote: "Since no grades were given students at the time of my Master's study, it would not have occurred to me to apply for a fellowship until the department head suggested such a procedure and thereby influenced the level of potential achievement."

A social worker: "College adviser who was the first person to discuss social work with me . . . [which turned out to be] just what I had been 'looking for.' " A statistician: "Undergraduate college physics professor persuaded me to go into graduate studies in statistics rather than physics or mathematics; he believed statistics offered a much better future for a girl. I believe he was right." A physician: "Professor M. of Department of Philosophy,——— College, taught Ethics and helped me rationalize my need for excellence and to integrate this with my need to assist the Negro community of which I am a member."

Although some received helpful guidance, others realized in retrospect that they had missed it: "I went to a very small country high school. . . . My mother . . . like many neighbors did not have great respect for higher education. . . . What I desperately needed was some wise counselor to encourage me 'to hitch my wagon to a star' and strive for the thing I really wanted. But no one did. . . . After floundering for years I finally aimed at librarianship and found it my ideal work."

A sociologist reported: "I limited myself too early too much. . . . I wish I had taken more languages, more science, more variety in college and graduate school. I wish I had become more of a specialist in something after acquiring a broader background." An historian who dropped out before taking her oral examinations for the doctorate: "It occurs to me that some kind of counseling on the campus would perhaps have shown me what I couldn't perceive myself. My graduate adviser . . . certainly tried to be helpful. But he was one of the very people whose very concern was making me feel more and more idiotic and embarrassed and making it all the harder for me to pass the orals. . . . Had I known of any disinterested person on campus whose function it was to hear and advise on such matters, I should have seen him early. As it was, I ended simply by running away."

Major external events such as World War II also have important effects for good or bad on the plans of young people. A librarian who remained single told us that her fiance had been killed in World War II. A physician recognized that "World War II undoubtedly broke down barriers against women in medicine." An economist said: "World War II unquestionably enabled me to obtain a better job at a higher salary immediately after college than would otherwise have been the case." A professor of English reported: "I interrupted my teaching to join the WAVES for two to three years. This was an interesting experience in itself, but chiefly because it provided the means for graduate school."

A financial management expert recalled: "I went into service which caused me to leave the Southern town in which I was born and raised. This changed my whole life." Although many others reported that their plans had been affected by World War II, perhaps the more striking finding is that many failed to note any effects from the war.

We asked the women if, while in graduate school, they had considered the possible problems that might arise if they sought to continue their careers after they married. In addition, we asked them how they had thought they would deal with these options and conflicts, if they should arise. Table 3.1 summarizes their responses. The one-quarter of the group who said that they were unaware of possible problems or had not even considered the question while in graduate school may have been following the rule of dealing with choices only when they arise. Similarly, those who did not answer this question did not concern themselves, at least consciously, with whether and when they would marry or with the possibility of a conflict between marriage and a career.

Of the two-thirds who realized that they might run into a problem, about half looked forward to resolving it in favor of either a career or marriage, while the others expected to combine work and marriage. A large number of those favoring marriage over a career expected only brief interruptions in their working lives for child rearing.

In summary of this aspect of their lives, most of the young women in our group were fortunate in having parents who had positive attitudes toward higher education for their daughters and who were able in many instances to

TABLE 3.1

Anticipated Solutions		*Percent*
Would favor career		17
career only; no mention of marriage	12	
restrict marriage in favor of career	5	
Would combine marriage and career		33
Would favor marriage		18
limit career in favor of marriage	7	
end career after marriage	11	
Did not consider problem		25
unaware of potential problems	13	
never gave thought to question	12	
No answer		7
Total		*100*

underwrite most or all of the expenditures involved. Many parents also had a positive attitude toward their daughters' preparing for a career. These young women were encouraged by their parents to make the most of their potential and to find the types of lives which would yield them the greatest satisfaction.

Most of these young women stayed in school long enough to acquire at least one graduate degree and a significant minority succeeded in earning a doctorate. Apparently, most of them enjoyed their studies. As their interests deepened, they sought to plan their lives so as to make use of what they had learned and had come to enjoy.

When they looked ahead, and most of them did, they realized that if they married they might have to do some juggling and balancing to bring their work and career goals into alignment with their marital and family responsibilities. But they were not disconcerted by anticipation of the future and the problems that it might bring.

4

Options and Decisions

Increasing affluence and the deepening of democratic values have many positive implications for the well-being of individuals but none more important than the extension of opportunities for individuals to pursue their own preferences and goals. A wealthy society makes it possible for young people to delay making crucial decisions until they have attained some degree of maturity and to make changes at a later date without prohibitive costs. And in a democratic society such as ours, young people are able to make their own plans to a great extent. The range of acceptable behavior and of acceptable patterns of life is substantial. Affluence and democracy broaden and deepen the range of choices open to individuals.

Broadened options are characteristic of almost every group in our society. This chapter will delineate the broad options that the young women in our group confronted at various stages of their development and will call attention to the points of similarity and difference between them and a corresponding group of men. Our aim is to develop a framework for describing the ways in which these young women made decisions with respect to three major areas of opportunity—marriage, family, and occupational endeavor—which are considered *in extenso* in the following chapters.

A young boy knows that he will have to work when he grows up. If one asks a boy of five what he wants to be, he will reply in terms of an occupation—aviator, fireman, doctor. He will not answer that he will be "a daddy." But if his sister is asked, she is likely to say that when she grows up, she will be "a mommy." Each is considered an acceptable response.

Young boys and girls think differently about work and these differences continue and sharpen as they reach adolescence and young adulthood. Every young man knows that he must become concerned about his occupational choice and its resolution. He knows that he must work, and work most of his life.

The parallel social expectation for a young woman is that she, on the other hand, will marry and raise a family. She may expect to work regularly or intermittently, full or part time, but she is not required to make her plans accordingly. Only if she remains single will society expect her to work, and if she belongs to that small minority who inherited money, even this requirement can be lifted. Not so in the case of a young man. Society does not care so much whether he marries—although most men do—but it expects him to hold down a job. And this requirement is independent of whether he has private means which would enable him to live without working.

Men have no option except to plan their lives around work. On the other hand women are free of this requirement. Their options are much broader. There is considerably more tolerance in our society for women who remain single than for men who remain idle.

What are the types and varieties of options which young women have? Although every woman does not have all of them, the following options do confront many.

The first major arena within which women have a great many choices is marriage and parenthood. While there is considerable pressure on all young women to marry and have a family, many who do not are able to shape meaningful and satisfying lives and command the respect and even the admiration of the larger society. In earlier generations the single woman had only narrow choices. She could remain at home and eventually take care of her parents or she could move in with a relative, where in return for room and board she might, and often did, serve as maid, cook, governess. If she sought to avoid the "charity" of her family she might enter a religious order. There were few alternatives.

Today the single woman can lead a very much fuller life than in the past. She can hold down a good job; she can have a nice home; she can enjoy the company of men without risk of criticism. Key to this altered position of the single woman are the greatly enlarged opportunities for women to prepare for, enter upon, and advance in many desirable occupational fields which provide both good income and considerable social prestige.

Some women remain single because they question whether they will be able to establish and maintain a continuing relationship with a man and therefore avoid the attempt. Others have other reasons for not marrying. Some have idealized standards for the men they want to marry. Some feel that marriage and a family might force them to alter their career plans. A small minority have serious questions about bringing children into a world that has demonstrated repeatedly its capacity for cruelty and destruction. More positively, a few with deep religious or moral conviction do not want a husband or children because they hope to find fulfillment and salvation in a life of good works. For any one of these or for still other reasons, women may decide not to marry.

Those women who do decide to marry have a second choice—as to the timing. While the prevailing romantic ideal of marriage holds that people should marry when they fall deeply in love, the values that people hold and the plans they have made condition their falling in love. Young women are likely at one time or another to confont situations where they must decide whether to marry or to postpone marriage. Those who are pursuing a carefully articulated educational and occupational plan are not likely to be so swept off their feet by a romantic attachment that they are unable to consider any other factor.

Even when a woman marries today, she has an option: if she finds her marriage intolerable, she can dissolve it. In earlier generations the woman who made a bad marriage was in an unfortunate situation. Divorce was very difficult, if not impossible. She had little prospect of supporting herself. Many women had to put up with unhappy marriages because they had no real alternative.

While divorce is still difficult, especially when young children are involved, the costs today often appear tolerable, especially for an educated woman who can look forward to working and perhaps to marrying again. Moreover, many unhappily married women can expect that, if they decide to obtain a divorce, their husbands will contribute substantially to the support of the children. Today, divorce is a realistic alternative to an unhappy marriage.

When a young woman marries, most people assume that she will have children. But some women decide not to. Those with strong career drives may not wish to be tied down; others may fear the responsibility of raising a family, or may simply not like children. Although some women who remain childless are unable to have children, for many others this is a reflection of choice, not infertility.

For the majority who do wish to have children, there is still considerable latitude with respect to timing and number. Since most women do not consider their marriages complete or their role as married women secure until they have children, they are likely to start their families shortly after they marry. Reenforcement of this trend comes from the dominant psychiatric doctrine that young parents make the best parents. Many young women complete their families by their middle twenties.

Yet, women have considerable choice about when to start and to complete their families. Educated women may make these decisions on the basis of the stage of their own education; they may decide largely in terms of their husbands' career; or they may consider how children would affect their own career, both in the near and more distant future. For many, the decision about when to have children involves many considerations.

We see then that the educated woman has great discretion with regard to whether to marry, when to marry, whether to seek a divorce if her marriage is unsuccessful, when to start having a family, the spacing of her children, and the number of children. In all of these crucial matters she has considerable freedom of choice.

The second major area of options is the work arena. The first and most important decision is whether to work at all, which, as we have said, is more a matter of personal choice than social determination. If she decides to work, she can still decide when to work. Another option is whether to work after marriage, and another is whether to work after starting a family. Some women decide that children need not affect their careers and continue to work during and after their childbearing years. At the opposite extreme are those who stop working when they marry and never return. Between these extremes are many who stop working for various lengths of time. Although our society still expects motherhood to take priority over working, the working mother is becoming more and more socially tolerated, particularly if she has a scarce or highly regarded skill.

A next major option is how much to work. While most men are under pressure and compulsion to hold down a full-time job, many women can choose to work a few hours a week or full time. Or they may decide to work full time for limited periods of the year.

Another option concerns money. Educated men are under considerable pressure to reach high-income levels, especially since the economic and social status of their family depends in considerable measure on their success in their occupational role. Married women are under much less pressure to maximize their income since their families are not usually dependent on their income. Therefore, more readily than men, they can accept a job for its intrinsic satisfaction with less reference to the external rewards.

Within the work area, then, women face a great many options: whether to work, when to work, how much to work, and with what intensity to pursue their career goals. Each of these options is broader than those which men with comparable education and ability have.

This brings us to another major area where women have wide options—their role in community activities. The American scene has long stressed the importance of voluntary efforts and women, particularly married women, have long played a major role in the organization and functioning of voluntary organizations.

Not long ago participation in community affairs was the only outlet outside of her home for a married woman. These community activities provided her with many of the satisfactions which are found on the job: companionship, the opportunity to participate in a common effort to accomplish a useful end, and the opportunity to achieve excellence, distinction, and sometimes even power. Today of course many women find these opportunities in the world of work. Voluntary activities are no longer the sole escape route from the home.

When a woman decides to volunteer her time and skill, she has many options. There are professional, religious, educational, political, health, and welfare organizations—truly scores of different organizations that welcome the volunteer. Her choice generally depends on which of these she believes can make the best use of her skills and which are closest to her interests.

She then must decide how much time to invest. She can be a dues-paying member and attend monthly meetings, or she may opt for a minor leadership part. She may decide to try for a key leadership role. It is well known that a few dedicated volunteer workers expend more time and energy for their organizations than do many women in full-time employment. In voluntary activities, as with her family and work, the educated woman has a great many options.

It should be noted, at least in passing, that a woman also has a choice of what to do with other leisure time. She can devote it to self-development through reading, taking courses, painting, or music. Or she may devote it to sports, card-playing, and similar activities. Whatever she does, here is one further area where she confronts options and can make decisions.

There are, of course, exaggerations in the foregoing scheme of multiple options. We know that there are many restrictions and limitations on the choices of all people. At this point, we will note the most important of these constraints for women. These are family responsibilities, the opportunities of the labor market, the social climate, and, most important, the factors contained in earlier decisions which are likely to exert a dominant influence on later choices.

On the whole, daughters have more obligations to their parents than do sons, and their patterns of life may be considerably influenced by their parents' needs and demands. A single woman is often called upon to take care of aged parents, as are married women although to a lesser extent.

More important, the margins of freedom of a married woman can be significantly affected by the occupational imperatives that govern her husband's life. In contemporary American society the man's work continues to take precedence and the woman's tends to be adjusted to his. Many women find themselves in communities where there is little or no prospect of their finding employment in their fields. Others are unable to hold a job because their husbands are shifted so frequently from one locale to another.

But marriage does not only constrict and limit a woman's freedom. If a man earns a high income it will be easier for his wife to secure competent household help if she wishes to work or participate in volunteer activities. Or, if her husband is in the same or cognate field, a woman may be able to work with him.

Although a husband may broaden or narrow a woman's margin of choice, children almost always narrow it. Preschool children need a great deal of attention and care, and it is often difficult for a woman to find a satisfactory substitute during the time that she is away from home.

The prevailing patterns of work also affect the options that women have. There are certain types of work, such as medical practice or editing, that women can carry on at home, and there are certain types of work for which employers prefer to hire women. Moreover, there are some fields which have had persistent shortages during the past two decades, such as teaching and nursing, and where it is, therefore, relatively easy for qualified women to secure employment. On the other hand, many employers balk at hiring women, particularly women who are unwilling to work full time. Rules prohibiting nepotism block many women in academic life—the institution at which a man teaches may preclude the employment of his wife. There are also state rules of licensure that put roadblocks in the path of many professionally trained women who have been forced to relocate. Moreover, many positions open to women carry such low wages that they do not provide enough compensation to cover the additional expenses connected with employment.

A woman's activities may be affected by the dominant attitudes of the community in which she lives. In many parts of the United States there are still strong objections when the mother of young children works. Moreover, the custom that women in middle- and upper-income families, especially in small communities, participate in various volunteer activities exerts a force in favor of such activity even if a woman would prefer paid employment.

This brings us to the last and perhaps the most powerful of the limitations. The choices that a woman makes at every point in time and the margins of freedom that she has with respect to them is greatly affected by the decisions she made earlier. A few illustrations can make this clear. A young woman may delay marriage so long that she restricts her options, and it may turn out that no suitable man crosses her path. Another may decide to have a large family, but after the arrival of her fourth child she finds her home and children quite burdensome.

In what respects are the options facing educated women unique to them? To some extent, educated men also have broadened options. For instance, young men may have a choice between completing their doctorates and early marriage. And educated men, like educated women, have to decide how much time and energy they are willing to invest in volunteer and leisure-time activities rather than in work or in shared family undertakings. Yet despite these and other parallels between the choice processes of men and women, fundamental differences can be identified which give unique shape and contour to the lives of educated women.

American society places great stress on "success." One of the major differences between the social roles of men and women are the areas in which they can be successful. A man achieves status almost exclusively through his work. Although a married woman's status is largely determined by her husband's, she retains considerable scope for self-determination. No one would dispute the success of a prominent professional woman. But the mother of three "wonderful" children, the wife of a prominent businessman, or the president of the League of Women Voters also have valid claims to success.

The educated woman has an opportunity to change her mind and her actions, not once, but repeatedly—often with little or no cost. In fact, a change in her circumstances—including the maturing of her children—implies that she must make new choices, since her former decisions no longer fit her situation. Between the ages of twenty-five and sixty-five most men find themselves in relatively narrow career grooves. They face options but most of them are within relatively narrow bounds. But within the first two decades of adulthood most educated women experience radical changes in their family situations. These changes encourage them to assess their new situations as they arise and make new choices.

The counterpart to facing choices is making decisions. We have seen that the educated woman makes decisions continuously. Moreover, she must make many of them without any directly relevant experience and sometimes without models from her parental home or from society at large. That is a result of revolution—the old models do not adequately fit the new situation.

The thrust of the following chapters is to elicit the facts about the many options that our group of educated women faced and to delineate the patterns that can be discerned in their decision-making. We will then be one step further toward understanding the impact of the revolutionary changes that are under way in our contemporary society on the life styles of educated women.

5

Family and Community

Every woman who has a home engages in "homemaking." A single woman may "keep house" for herself alone, or for herself and one or both parents, or she may share housekeeping or homemaking responsibilities with a friend. For most single women, however, homemaking activities are secondary to their work. But for the wife and mother, housekeeping and the care of children are her primary responsibilities, and these functions are likely to occupy a considerable part of her time and energy, sometimes preempting all of her interest and concern. If a woman has many children and especially, if they are young, it is likely that homemaking is the major focus of her life. In light of what we already know about the background and education of the women in our group, however, we would expect to find that most of them want to engage in some activity outside of the home, be it community affairs or paid employment even when they have young children.

This chapter will describe their activities within the family and in the community—that is, the non-job aspects of their lives. Subsequent chapters will be concerned with their participation in the world of work. We will first describe their marital status and the number of their children in order to understand the importance of family and community in the patterning of their lives.

Of the 311 women in our group, 88, or 28 percent, never married, and of the 223 who married, 39, or 17 percent, had no children. The proportion of single women in our group is much higher than in the population as a whole, where among women in approximately the same age brackets only about 6 percent are single. This means that the proportion of single women in our group was more than 4½ times that in the general population. The proportion of childless married women in our group was slightly, but not conspicuously, above the national norm.

Ours was a group who married relatively late. Only 6 percent were married in their teens and about one-quarter did not marry until they were twenty-nine or older. Nevertheless only half of the group who eventually had children had their first child within the first two years of marriage. Of the remainder, about half waited between three to five years, and about half waited even longer before having their first child.

In summary: 28 percent were single; 13 percent of those married had no children; and of the 59 percent with children, about one-third had children below the age of four; and about two-thirds had children younger than eight. In fact, nine women were pregnant at the time they returned the questionnaire. In only a relatively few families—20 out of the 184 with children, or 11 percent—was the youngest child at least of junior-high-school age.

Since there are many ways in which motherhood can affect a woman's career, variations for the same woman as well as among different women, we found that the simplest way to describe the behavior of these mothers was to determine the *earliest* point at which a woman returned to work after the birth of any of her children. For example, if a woman remained out of the labor force for five years following the birth of one child but only three years following the birth of another, we classified her as returning to work three years after the birth of a child.

Of all the women who had children, 19 percent, or almost one-fifth, returned to work while one of their children was an infant. A much larger group, 39 percent, or almost two-fifths, returned to work when a child was between one and four years old. The third group, totaling about 16 percent, did not return until a child was five or older. The last group (26 percent) has not yet returned to work; half of these women have at least one child under five years old and half have older children.

Another way of reading these data is to say that 74 percent of these women returned to work after having children and of these almost 80 percent returned when their youngest child was less than five years old. The striking finding is that although the birth of a child increases a woman's involvement with the home and family, most of our women withdrew from the labor force for a comparatively short period of time.

This is how some of the women discussed the problems which they faced after they had children. A college teacher of chemistry said: "When my first child was born, my husband was just getting started, so I decided to continue working." Another academic wrote: "I suspect . . . that a new trend is developing. I myself worked through two pregnancies and others are doing the same. The very acceptance of pregnant women in schools and on jobs combined with the increasing popularity and success of nursery schools seems to indicate that women can combine homemaking with other activities during the years when family obligations are heaviest." Support for this "new trend" comes from another teacher and college administrator who reported: "I have been working on in school without break since 1943. I worked 'til the day my two children were born and was out two weeks following each."

Others felt very strongly that the arrival of a baby was no reason for a woman fundamentally to reorganize her way of life. A medical research scientist had this to say: "To the best of my knowledge, having a baby does not reduce the number of neurons in the 'thinking apparatus'. . . . Not being with a small child all day made it much easier for me to be reasonable and patient and understanding of his needs and his behavior. I admit that I curtailed other activities when he was very young so I could play with him. I might also add that I was often physically tired."

But this was only one side of the story. The "homemakers" also held strong views. A respondent who had four children said: "Children's needs are the dominant influence requiring my presence at home almost continually while infants, the greater proportion of the time during preschool years, at least after school during school years, and again almost continually during the summer. This, plus continued need for supervision during high-school years and lack of availability of intelligent and competent mother-substitutes, would seem to preclude pursuit of a full-time outside career and makes even a part-time one very difficult under present employment conditions. Obsolescence of knowledge during the years spent at home multiplies the difficulty."

Another, a mother of three, argued: "It doesn't make much sense to me to prepare oneself intellectually and culturally and then relegate one's own children to an environment much inferior to that which you can supply, e.g., leisure time guidance, reading activities, ethical values, morals, proper nutrition, discipline." The same viewpoint was put in more general terms by a mother of two who stayed home while her children were young but went back to work to pay her son's tuition at private school: "I think that marriage, homemaking and child rearing are a woman's natural functions in this world and I feel that I am fulfilling my destiny."

Others held less sharp ideological positions but believed that women should stop working when they had small children at home. One of these recognized that "there are exceptional women who can pursue a career and still maintain a normal, healthy family circle but they *are* exceptional and should be considered as such."

The degree to which these women devoted their time and energy to homemaking, including child rearing, was undoubtedly influenced by the satisfaction which they derived from these functions. Table 5.1 summarizes the replies of the respondents to our question about which were the most and which the least gratifying aspects of homemaking. It should be noted in passing that a high proportion of the single women apparently did not think that they were expected to answer this question and therefore did not reply. Those who replied made 353 positive statements about homemaking and 270 negative statements.

By far the most important source of satisfaction in homemaking for most of these women was "Personal relations" with husband and children. The more children a woman had the more likely she was to find her major satisfaction in

TABLE 5.1

Source of Gratification	*Degree of Gratification (in percent)* most	least
Nature of activity	33	67
Self-realization	7	5
Personal relations and child rearing	44	9
Social service and significance	8	1
Conditions of housekeeping	8	18
Total	*100*	*100*

these relationships. A significant minority reported that they found their principal satisfactions in the nature of the activities, particularly the creative ones like cooking or entertaining. Only a small minority, however, considered homemaking a principal avenue for "self-realization." These were primarily mothers of large families.

One interesting interpretation can be made from the finding that the satisfactions which these women derived from homemaking increased with the size of their family. The fact that mothers of large families were more likely to stay home and care for their children may reflect not only the demands made on them but also their desire to have and care for large families.

The following quotations indicate the depth and range of gratifications that many women derive from homemaking and child rearing. A single librarian commented on the gratification which she had from "making a pleasant comfortable home for my father." A married government official without children wrote that "the creation of an attractive home which is the expression of your tastes and individuality, one in which your family can be comfortable and happy" was a major source of gratification for her.

As we might have anticipated, several women singled out their activities with their children as the high-point of their homemaking. A mother of three said: "Bringing up children—ours are the type that recite poetry, dance, are musically talented, get straight A's, all in addition to playing cops-and-robbers, building shacks, etc.—I hardly feel my education wasted."

Helping her husband was an important element for a former teacher, a mother of two who mentioned trying to "lessen my husband's tensions." Other women called attention to the conditions associated with homemaking: "You are your own boss and have your own hours—even though they are long."

Not surprisingly, most women reported as the least gratifying aspects of homemaking the routine housekeeping chores which they found onerous because they were so demanding and there was so little scope for the use of talent or skill. A mother of three, who was employed as an accountant until her first pregnancy, mentioned the lack of opportunity for self-realization. "The feeling that there is very little concrete to show for your time spent—so many activities are done every day and need redoing almost as soon as you have finished." The "lack of intellectual stimulation" was a frequent source of discontent. An unusual comment was that of a widow with three children who felt that the "children's errors or family's may reflect my failure as a mother."

Several single women complained that their homemaking left much to be desired because they didn't have "a mate to share it with." Other complaints from those who were married and had children included the "lack of affection, recognition, and respect for one's efforts." The time pressure was also a cause of discontent: A mother of three quoted: "Women's work is never done!"

In addition to homemaking there is another non-job activity which is important for many women—voluntary activities in their communities. A first consideration is the amount of time these women spend in these activities. Twenty-one percent reported that they did not participate at all in volunteer activities. This means that 79 percent had some involvement, even if small. This is a large proportion compared to the national figure of 51 percent who engage in volunteer activities. In our group, about 20 percent reported participation of approximately one hour or less per week, and another 33 percent said they spent between two and five hours weekly. Eighteen percent reported spending more than five hours a week on volunteer activities. We have no information about the extent of the participation of 8 percent.

According to a recent national survey, the average volunteer worker devotes about two hours a week to her organizations; in comparison to this average, our women are more heavily involved. Nevertheless, these weekly hours are far less than what employed women would spend on even a part-time job.

We related the level of participation in voluntary activities with the marital status of the respondents and the size of the community in which they lived. Of the three subgroups, single women, married women without children, and married women with children, the last had the highest rate of participation. As we will see, most of these women were not holding full-time jobs. With respect to location, those living in suburbs and small towns were twice as likely as those living in metropolitan centers to participate in voluntary activities. Moreover, they were more likely to devote considerably more time—six or more hours weekly—to these activities than were urban dwellers.

We asked the respondents to tell us their reasons for engaging in voluntary activities. The three principal reasons were the social significance of the work, the nature of the activity, and association with others. In light of the widespread belief that voluntary activities provide many women with a constructive outlet for their talents and energy comparable to what they can find in paid employment, we should note that only a very small number—3 percent—indicated that they sought self-realization through participation in voluntary activities.

Our women engage in volunteer activities which are related to the other facets of their lives. The most popular type of volunteer activity is that connected with a professional society—a reflection of their education and present working status. However, practically no full-time homemakers belong to professional societies. With regard to other organizations, the allegiance of the women is more or less evenly divided among religious and ethnical groups, civic and political organizations, and educational and youth organizations. The smallest number are involved with health and welfare organizations. About half of the respondents are active in more than one organization.

The following quotations show the range of factors that motivated various women to engage in unpaid work. A white respondent living in the Deep South wrote: "I felt strongly the need for civil rights for everyone; I also felt that public schools should not be sacrificed because of prejudices of others." Another wrote: "I enjoy working with people. I like making up programs, teaching, and so forth; and I also thought it would help my husband's practice (optometrist)." A third, a scientist with four children, said that her motivation was "partly interest, partly necessity of getting away from purely domestic activities." An honest soul admitted: "I participated mainly because of interest but, to some extent, I did so because of my inability to say no when asked to join committees or organizations."

Several mothers mentioned the factor of civic obligations. "I wanted to feel I was 'paying my way' since my children enjoyed the benefits of belonging to Cubs and the Sunday School." Another said: "In general, I had a desire to be a responsible citizen. The political candidates I've worked for have usually lost, but it feels good to try." The wife of a public utility president reported: "Some participation [is] required by local mores and customs." Another stated: "I generally became involved through some facet of my everyday life, i.e., a child became old enough to go to nursery school or grade school; psychiatrists' wives were encouraged to join auxiliaries, etc. Politics is a real pet interest of mine."

Once these women joined such organizations as volunteer groups, they experienced varying types of satisfaction from their participation. Their principal gratifications came from their awareness that what they were doing had social significance, and they also enjoyed the interpersonal contacts. In contrast to its importance as a factor which influenced them to participate in volunteer work in the first place, the nature of the activity is not mentioned as a source of major gratification.

The reverse was true with regard to the aspect of self-realization, which had not been an important stimulus to participation but turned out to be important as a source of satisfaction. As a matter of fact, a reenforcement principle was at work: those who found self-realization through volunteer activity were those who devoted considerable time and energy to this sphere of their lives.

The following quotations indicate the satisfactions which these women derived from participation as a volunteer. "Having spent six years in a country (Italy) where grass-roots democracy is almost unknown, I began to appreciate anew the value of our political clubs, Kiwanis, and Rotary, PTA, League of Women Voters, etc. When those pursuits are undertaken with the same energy and thought and utilization of skill and training as in a salaried job, I think they can provide a great deal of satisfaction and feeling of contribution."

A social scientist, with three children said: "Like paid work, the most gratifying aspect of volunteer activity is the fulfillment of the urge to creativity and accomplishment, of making one's unique contribution." Another respondent stressed diversity: "Each organization is so different—but generally I enjoy defining the problems, then getting involved in active programs to meet the problems. I also like the contact with diverse groups of well informed interesting people." Some women saw professional gains: "I feel like I'm 'keeping my hand in' my profession and volunteers are essential to those organizations to which I feel closest."

Negative comments about their volunteer activities were elicited from about 2 out of every 3 women in the group. Their objections were widely different but many complained about the nature of the work and the absence of satisfying interpersonal relations. It appears then that two of the major goals sought from participation in volunteer activities were not met.

One type of dissatisfaction is indicated by the following brief comments: "People appreciate what they pay for—therefore show lack of enthusiasm for work put out by well-intentioned volunteers." Or: "Volunteer activities do not take the place of paid *responsible* employment." Or: "As far as I am concerned, volunteer activity is 'made' work, having little real importance or significance except for the person directly involved."

Some pointed to other sources of dissatisfaction: "The terrible hours, the in-fighting, the door slammed in your face, and wasted time—the disorderliness which is necessary for success." A medical scientist objected to "not being accepted as a professional with special knowledge—working below one's training and experience." One wrote: "Sometimes the activity becomes an end in itself and really fails to accomplish any purpose other than time-filling." Another respondent said that volunteer work had many drawbacks: "Wasted time, 'nudnicks,' pressures of extraneous detail, personality coddling, sacrificing time from family, sleep, and reading." Another remarked: "I detest the interpersonal 'nonsense' which goes on in many women's groups." The range and intensity of these dissatisfactions shows that, despite the fact that a large number of our women gave some time to one organization or another, these activities provide only limited satisfaction for highly educated women. The acerbity of the foregoing quotations indicate that although the role of the volunteer offered a significant challenge to some women, it had little to offer to many others.

All of our women had some amount of leisure time during which they engaged in a variety of activities. Most often reported was their active or passive participation in cultural and creative activities such as art, music, and the crafts. Sports were an important attraction, and all of the group spent some time in social activities.

The women reported on their leisure-time activities in many ways: "I read to keep alive above the neck." "Reading restoreth my soul." "I can become totally engrossed in art; it requires no other participants." A former English major, now at home caring for two children, commented: "Writing seems to give life some meaning." A mother of four who engaged in swimming, reading, drama, attendance at concerts, writing poetry, remarked: "These are my rewards for being good."

Some responses were more unusual. A newly married writer said: "Being romantically in love, all leisure activities—including even some conventional hobbies—have centered around the act of love and the spirit of loving." A mother of two who had stopped working, said: "The many pressures of jobs and civic activities resulted for me in such constant activity that I often felt I lacked the chance to grow within and to achieve the kind of personal development I would have liked—reading, thinking, 'being' instead of 'doing.' Now with more leisure I am intrigued with the challenge of growth and use of leisure creatively."

Some were caustic: "With five children?!" Another, with two children and a full-time job, wrote: "I do not know what is meant by leisure time. I swim. Occasionally, I have bowled. Primarily I read, sew, garden, work, iron, mend, clean during leisure hours. Sometimes I sleep."

Leisure-time activities appear to play much the same role in the lives of these educated women as for other women. They help to fill time, they provide opportunities for self-development, and they are an arena for family enrichment.

Now that we have reviewed their activities with respect to their families, volunteer organizations, and leisure-time pursuits, we are in a position to draw some tentative generalizations about the significance of these spheres for their lives and satisfactions. For the more than 70 percent who were married, and particularly for the 60 percent who had children, their families served as a major focus of their interest and activities and in turn offered them important satisfactions. But only a small minority found their homemaking and child-rearing functions—even when supplemented by volunteer and leisure-time activities—completely satisfying. This helps to explain why so many are involved in the world of work and why most of those who are currently directing themselves exclusively to homemaking plan eventually to return to work.

6

Work and Careers

Work plays a key role in the lives of these educated women and merits careful appraisal. In this chapter, we will assess its influence from two approaches: first, to review the part that work currently plays in the lives of these women; and second, to review on a longitudinal axis the part that work has played since they were in graduate school.

Since work is only one of the areas of life to which these women devote time and energy and from which they seek gratifications, we will first set their occupational activities within the framework of their total activities, which include homemaking and voluntary participation in charitable and other organizations. The major roles which they play today are set out in Table 6.1. "Full-time employment" refers to those women whose participation in homemaking or in voluntary activities is small. Those who engage in "outside activities" spend at least ten hours weekly on undertakings other than homemaking or a job, that is, on voluntary activities or on further education. Those engaged in any "homemaking" have young children at home. The tabulation indicates that 3 out of 4 of our women are working either full or part time, and that of the quarter who are at home, 1 out of 3 engages in considerable outside activity.

Table 6.2 shows the hours per week worked by the 226 women who are employed. This distribution tells us that

TABLE 6.1

Role		*Percent*
Worker		62
full-time employment	36	
full-time employment and outside activities	5	
full-time employment and homemaking	21	
Combination (part-time worker and homemaker)		13
Homemaker		25
homemaking only	17	
homemaking and outside activities	8	
Total		*100*

most of those who work, even the part-time workers, spend many hours per week at their jobs, and of those who work full time, over thirty-five hours weekly, many put in long hours.

TABLE 6.2

Hours	*Percent*
5 or less	1
6–15	8
16–25	9
26–35	5
36–45	57
46 or more	20
Total (N = 226)	*100*

Tables 6.3 to 6.6 set forth the fields in which our women work, the functions which they perform, and the sector of

the economy in which they are employed. Those who are presently undertaking further education are included in Table 6.3, which covers 74 percent of the entire group. Only 1 out of 4 was at home, participating neither in paid employment nor in study.

TABLE 6.3

Field	*Percent*
Humanities	18
Social Sciences	13
Natural Sciences	11
Medicine or law	11
Social Work or public health	18
Journalism or business	10
Education or library science	19
Total (N = 232)	*100*

The functions that these women perform and the type of institutions in which they are employed are set out in Table 6.4. Elementary and high-school teachers have been classified as holding staff positions. A considerable proportion of the group are in fields and performing functions where the conditions of employment do not require a full nine-to-five day for forty-eight or more weeks in the year, such as school teachers and those who hold appointments on a college or university faculty. The small proportion employed in the profit sector of the economy is a reflection not so much of the fact that these are women, as of their educational background and occupational preferences. A high proportion of all highly educated individuals, male as well as female, work in the not-for-profit sector, that is, for government or nonprofit organizations. The major exceptions are engineers, natural scientists, particularly chemists, and those in medicine or law. But women are relatively underrepresented in those professions, to some extent because their vocational choices reflect their recognition of business' reluctance to hire females.

TABLE 6.4

Function	*Percent*
University teaching	31
Research	11
Administration: government or nonprofit	16
Staff positions: government or nonprofit	25
Administration or staff: business	8
Self-employment: professional and other	9
Total (N = 226)	*100*

Table 6.5 sets forth the interrelationship between the fields in which our group specialize, and the functions which they perform in their jobs. The functions which they perform or the sectors in which they are employed and their fields of specialization are significantly related: university teaching with the humanities; research with the natural and social sciences; self-employment with medicine and law; profit-making enterprises with business and journalism; and nonprofit organizations with the four classic female professions—education, library service, social work, and public health.

In addition to considering their present roles and work participation, we want to consider their experiences in the labor market since they first began to work. To this end we will review the proportion of their adult lives that they have worked, the history of their labor force participation, and the pattern of their careers.

Although this is a relatively young group—3 out of 4 are younger than forty-four—most of its members have spent

TABLE 6.5

	Function or Sector						
Field	*university teaching*	*research*	*administration* *	*staff* *	*business*	*self-employed*	*student*
Humanities	31	0	1	4	2	2	1
Social Sciences	8	8	3	6	0	2	3
Natural Sciences	11	9	2	1	0	1	0
Medicine or law	3	2	4	9	1	7	1
Social Work or public health	6	4	13	15	0	1	0
Journalism or business	1	1	2	0	13	5	0
Education or library science	10	0	12	20	1	2	1
Total (N = 232)	*70*	*24*	*37*	*55*	*17*	*20*	*6*

* Nonprofit.

a considerable number of years in the labor force. More than a third have been in the labor force for over seventeen years and more than one-half for at least thirteen years. Only a very small number, less than 2 percent, have never had a job. In consonance with established practice, we have counted a woman as a member of the labor force if she held any type of job for any length of time during the course of a calendar year. A more refined measure of the extent to which these women work is had when we give part-time work its proper weight as a proportion of full-time. When this is done, we find that over half of all the women in our group have worked between 80 and 100 percent of all their adult years, excluding time spent in school. On this basis, 70 percent of the group have worked at least 50 percent of their adult lives. Less than a third of the group have spent under 50 percent of their time at work.

These women did not work sporadically, or for a few hours a week. If time is a valid measure, we can say that work has played an important part in their lives.

Table 6.6 presents a percentage distribution of the work histories of the 311 women. A "continuous" work history

TABLE 6.6

Work History	*Percent*
Continuous	36
Minor breaks	14
Intermittent	12
Periodic	14
Terminated, temporarily or permanently	13
Minor or none	11
Total	*100*

describes those who have held full-time jobs throughout their adult lives. Those with "minor breaks" are full-time workers who have interrupted their careers for short intervals during which, however, some of them worked part time. The group with an "intermittent" work history has spent three or more short periods away from work or were part-time workers, only. The "periodic" group has dropped out of work one or more times, and each time for three or more years. Those who "terminated" left the labor market after a substantial period of work and have not yet returned to work. And those with a work history classified as "minor or none" have had less than four years in the labor force or have had no work experience at all.

We see that if minor interruptions are disregarded, half of the group has had a continuous work history, slightly over a quarter have been in and away from work throughout their adult lives, and only 11 percent never really got started on careers.

An interesting point that arises is the extent to which women who pursued different types of graduate studies are more or less likely to work in the same field, change fields, or stop working. Table 6.7 provides these data.

TABLE 6.7

Field of Graduate Study (in percent)

Field of Work	*humanities*	*social sciences*	*natural sciences*	*medicine, law*	*business, journalism*	*education, library science*	*public health, social work*
Same	61	48	73	78	28	58	50
Changed	20	27	6	4	32	19	17
Not working	19	25	21	18	40	23	33
Total	*100*	*100*	*100*	*100*	*100*	*100*	*100*

This is a crucial table and warrants close inspection. It shows, first, that those women who studied law or medicine and who obtained their degrees were most likely to remain in the labor market and to work in their chosen fields. Apparently, they were strongly motivated to pursue a career. Much the same pattern holds for those who specialized in the natural sciences. Another element in their career development is the fact that both of these groups entered a domain in which men predominate. The highest proportion who have stopped working are those who pursued graduate work in business or journalism. These fields too are dominated by men, but graduate courses in these fields are much less taxing than medicine or the natural sciences and therefore did not screen out those women with weak commitments.

One other broad deduction can be extracted. The likelihood that a woman will change her field of work is also related significantly to the subject of her specialization. Those who had majored in business or journalism were eight times more likely to change their field of employment than were those who had studied medicine or law. The social scientists were more than four times as likely to change their field as the natural scientists.

With regard to the relationship of functions to work histories, we find that those in administration and university teaching were more likely to have had a continuous work history, while those in research or in business tend to have had a broken career. While it is possible for a woman with heavy commitments at home to hold down an academic job because of the flexible hours and the long summer vacation, the only way that a woman can hold an administrative position or become successful as a self-employed professional is through full-time, full-year work.

So far we have looked only at the way in which the fields in which these women have been working and the functions which they have performed are related to their work patterns. But there were other equally important determinants. Key among them are the level of education which our women had acquired and their family situations. Table 6.8 provides an overview in percent of the relationships between the highest degree achieved and their present roles. Because of the small number, six, who did not acquire more than a baccalaureate degree, our comparison will concern the other two groups. Those with doctorates were much more likely to be working full time. The degree of investment in preparation appears to be an important determinant of commitment to work.

TABLE 6.8

	Degree (*in percent*)		
Role	*doctorate*	*masters or equivalent*	*baccalaureate*
Worker	86	48	66
Combination	7	16	17
Homemaker	7	36	17
Total	*100*	*100*	*100*

Table 6.9 indicates the extent to which motherhood and the number of children is related to whether these women work full time, part time, or not at all. The data reinforce what has been suggested earlier—that a woman's work history is greatly affected by the number of children she has. We find a strong direct relationship. With every increase in family size, there is a decrease in continuous participation in work. Even without children, a married woman is less likely to work continuously than a single woman. If a woman has one child, the chances are about even that she will have a continuous work history; if she has two children, the chances are two to one that she will not have a continuous work history. If she has three or more children, the probabilities against her continuing to work are overwhelming. In fact, over half of this latter group have dropped out of the labor force completely.

Marriage and children can have one of two kinds of effects on a woman's career. On the one hand, marriage usually *enables* her to drop out of the labor force if and when she desires. On the other hand, it may *force* her to drop out because of her husband's career or her responsibilities to her children. The similarity of the percentages between single women and married women without children points to the strong work orientation of our group. There was a difference of only 8 percent in career continuity between the two. The radical drop in continuous employment comes with one child and continues to drop with every additional child. It appears then that children are the

TABLE 6.9

	Family Situation (in percent)				
Work History	*single*	*married, no children*	*one child*	*two children*	*three or more children*
Continuous	91	83	48	29	7
Broken	7	15	29	39	40
Terminated, temporary or permanent	2	2	23	32	53
Total	*100*	*100*	*100*	*100*	*100*

primary factor influencing a woman's work decisions; frequently, their arrival prevents her continuous participation as a member of the work force.

In the preceding chapter, we looked for a relationship between the size of the communities in which our women live and their participation in voluntary activities and we found that there is a relationship. Now we must look at the relationship between their present roles and size of their communities. Table 6.10 shows that those who work full time are likely to live in urban centers, while those who are homemakers are more likely to be living in the suburbs or in small communities. But we are unable to determine whether those living in the suburbs are no longer interested in working or whether their living there makes it difficult for them to find suitable employment. Presumably both factors—where they live and their degree of interest in working—help to determine whether they are job holders.

We developed a three-way table to explore the interrelations of the number of children, family location, and the woman's present role, and found that if a woman has one or two children, location is an important independent variable affecting her present role. But once a woman has three or more children, this circumstance outweighs all others in determining whether or not she works.

TABLE 6.10

Size of Community (in percent)

Role	*metropolis*	*other city*	*suburb*	*small town*
Worker	82	67	49	50
Combination	9	14	12	14
Homemaker	9	19	39	36
Total	*100*	*100*	*100*	*100*

We explored still another relationship, that between husband's income and the woman's present role. While those whose husbands earn under $10,000 are somewhat more likely to work full time than those whose husbands earn over $15,000 and, conversely, those whose husbands are in the higher income brackets are more likely to be primarily homemakers than the wives of the low earners, the differences are not sharp.

Within wide margins, these women were able to choose a style of life. We will therefore review whether the anticipations which they held in graduate school about a future career and family were related significantly to what actually occurred. The questionnaire asked whether they had anticipated problems in combining marriage with a career and how they had intended to resolve them. We can see the impact of anticipation on later resolution in Table 6.11. Those who anticipated that their careers would take precedence over marriage and family largely followed through on their plans and now work full time, while those who did not think they could fit family and career together spent the least time in work.

The data indicate that a woman's involvement in work will be determined first by her family situation and second by such factors as her educational achievement, her field of specialization, her location, and her career plans.

TABLE 6.11

	Anticipations (in percent)			
Proportion of Working Life Spent at Work	*career take precedence*	*combination*	*family take precedence*	*did not consider possible conflict*
80–100	69	50	27	59
40–79	18	27	39	23
0–39	13	23	34	18
Total	*100*	*100*	*100*	*100*

This is how the women talked about their jobs and careers. A mother of six children who now has a government position as a mathematical statistician and who has worked continuously throughout her adult life put the matter very simply: "I feel I must work to express myself regardless of my children's needs." Much the same sentiment comes through the following comment which was written by an academician, a mother of three: "I know myself well enough to realize that I would work regardless of whether

I was paid or not. I am not happy when I am not working."

Another strongly affirmative view was expressed by a part-time journalist: "I consider myself fortunate that I never dread the coming of a working day—that I always look forward to it, that there is always something new awaiting me, and that when I come home my two-year-old is standing at the door—with a big grin on his face." A woman who had been home for ten years with three children before she returned to work reported: "I am a far happier person working than I was during the years I stayed home. . . . I am a person who enjoys working, studying, being busy."

A woman with a Ph.D. in chemistry who stayed out of the labor force for six years while her children were young, but who has been working in recent years reflected: "I enjoy my work and would be miserable sitting around doing nothing. It is cruel to forbid married women to work!"

A professor of foreign languages saw advantages to being out of the house much of the day: "My children benefit by being with an older woman during my absence and also from my better temper and attitude toward them when I am home." The epitome of this position is the following recital by a social scientist: "I have two children, one husband, a large house, a full-time professional job, and I turn out an average of three scientific articles a year. In short, I'm busy as hell. On the other hand, I'm a lot happier (in my own estimation) than women who play bridge, belong to PTA, collect for charities, and bake bread."

We have traced the way in which these women dealt with their options with respect to work. We found that most of them were sufficiently interested in working to spend a major portion of their adult life at it. Only a minority had loose or no ties to the world of work. These considerations bring us now to examining the sources of satisfaction and dissatisfaction which they derived from being employed.

We made use of the same category scheme that we had used earlier to study homemaking and volunteer activities, differentiating among the nature of the activity, opportunities for self-realization, interpersonal satisfactions, social significance, and conditions.

This is how the women talked about the nature of their work as the most gratifying aspect. A librarian reported: "I enjoy all aspects of my work," while a foreign language professor wrote "I like particularly the class hour in literature courses, and in a different way the time spent on research."

The element of self-realization comes through sharply in the following quotes. A public health professional commented: "The feeling of self-esteem, being capable, and being able to compete in a so-called man's world." A medical researcher specified: "Finding new facts in the laboratory —Discovery!" An unmarried social worker wrote about "the opportunity for sublimation and compensation for otherwise unmet needs of a woman."

The interpersonal aspects were selected by a professional in the health field who said: "The opportunity to meet, know, and work with some of the top-notch people in the hospital field." A language professor commented that the most gratifying aspect was her "relationship with other teachers and students."

The social significance and service aspects are mentioned

by a social worker, who wrote about her "feeling that I have in some way helped my client with his particular problem. This is both ego satisfaction and altruism." A government official remarked: "I like being involved in a small way in a major issue of the day."

Others stressed conditions and rewards as the principal source of their gratification. A divorced physician, currently an administrator on a hospital staff, said that the most gratifying aspect was "money and independence." A research assistant reported that she was interested in her "semimonthly pay check." Another: "I've never run a big law office before—and I'm enjoying the sheer 'status' of the job."

The members of our group also identified the least gratifying aspects of their work. Several in academic life called attention to disappointments in the nature of their work: "Committee meetings, staff meetings, making decisions which can equally be made by secretarial help." A physicist called attention to "the inhumanity of pure science." A researcher remarked on the problems engendered for her by the "occasional necessity to refuse to participate in projects which are not of interest to me."

Others found that their work did not provide them with opportunities for self-realization or interpersonal satisfactions. A Ph.D. in the humanities complained: "My present job of proofreading is far below my capabilities and training and holds no emotional satisfactions." A journalist called attention to "office politics, watching the men I work with jockey for promotion, trying to keep out of the fray." A librarian wrote: "As I have moved into administration I have become more removed from service to the public so that I have less and less of the work that made library service attractive to me." A teacher complained about the "university's attitudes toward the teaching profession—a kind of 'built-in' all-day baby-sitter!"

The lack of social significance and the unsatisfactory conditions of work were also singled out as major sources of dissatisfaction. A medical researcher commented: "There is no one thing I can single out unless it be the overall picture that I am not making any particular contribution to the world—but how many people really do?" And a lawyer complained about "doing nothing more significant than making rich people richer." A social worker called attention to "the limitations and frustrations in the helping process."

Others wrote about the adverse conditions affecting employment. One respondent wrote about the "long drive in heavy traffic, separation from children, just tired with home duties after day's work." A physician mentioned her discontent about "working for a salary and being dependent on an institution. Like most M.D.'s I would probably prefer the independence of private practice." An academician was unhappy about "the fact that I haven't tenure yet." A musicologist who liked her work had no complaints "except sometimes wishing for a higher salary."

These favorable and unfavorable responses to the work experience can be summarized. The largest proportion of the women singled out the social significance of their work and the nature of the work activity as the most important sources of satisfaction; opportunities for self-realization and interpersonal relations were also important. Only a minority mentioned the conditions of work—income and prestige—as important in yielding satisfactions. Of the unfavorable responses, complaints about particular aspects of work loomed largest with dissatisfactions with conditions coming next. There were about 50 percent more favorable responses than negative remarks.

We were able to classify the women in our group according to the following four career patterns: straight, broad, changed, and variant.

The successive jobs that a person holds are likely to be related. Some people start in one field and remain in it throughout all of their working lives. Others broaden out within the same general area. Still others make a more or less radical shift at some time in their careers. And still others just jump from job to job with very little direction or progression.

About a quarter of the entire group had a *straight* career pattern. Their careers have been marked by consistency, continuity, and progression within the same field. An example is a respondent who has been in the private practice of medicine for the past seven years, following her graduation from medical school and her postgraduate training. Another is a woman who has always pursued social casework despite repeated interruptions. She had to interrupt her education when her mother's death forced her to drop out of graduate school for two years to work. After receiving her M.S., she was again employed as a social worker. Although she dropped out of the labor force after the birth of each of her two children, she returned to social work after some time. At present, she has a part-time job as a caseworker and intends to continue at this job.

A somewhat greater proportion, roughly one-third, follow a *broad* pattern, that is, they have remained within their original area of work but have shifted either in terms of field or function. One example is another social worker who began as a caseworker, became a consultant to various agencies, and then moved over to a responsible teaching position in social work. She was widowed during the war and has one child. "I was first interested in teaching partly because of the free summer months it afforded me during my child's early years."

Another illustration of the broad pattern is one of the older respondents who, after graduating from college in 1938, worked as a clerk for two years in order to earn enough to continue her education. By 1941, she had secured a master's degree in public health. For the next two years, she worked as a laboratory assistant and a bacteriologist, again with an eye to accumulating savings in order to return to school. In 1943, she entered medical school and graduated three years later under the accelerated wartime program. After internship and residency, she became a physician in private practice. She is now on the staff of a major university teaching hospital and has a federal research grant.

Those with *changed* career patterns differ from the preceding groups in that their work experience is characterized by discontinuity. They changed their fields and/or functions and their later choices have no direct relation to their previous ones. About 25 percent fall into this pattern.

An example is a woman who took her master's degree in journalism and then worked for a few years in a news service, but did not find it as interesting or satisfying as she had expected. She therefore enrolled in divinity school and received her bachelor of divinity degree nine years after having acquired her master's degree in journalism. Since then, she has been engaged in student personnel work and religious leadership activities under the sponsorship of the YMCA.

A second is a woman who took her master's degree in economics in 1946 and worked in the field for several years until she married. She spent the next seven years at home taking care of her two young children. In 1954, in response to her husband's promptings, she entered law school, which had been her original goal but from which she had been deflected by her parents. After earning her LL.B. she established her own practice in which she is currently engaged.

The pattern of change was usually followed by women who discovered that they had entered a field of work which was wrong for them and who had the energy and desire to correct their mistake, by those who were blocked from pursuing their first choice, and by those who discovered that the circumstances of their lives—particularly marriage and children—made it exceedingly difficult if not impossible to stay within their chosen field. If they wanted to work, they had to find a more suitable occupation.

As suggested earlier, the concept of career development carries with it some sense of purposefulness, direction, and progression. However, some individuals find it difficult to get started; others find it difficult to make perceptible progress. Those who convey the impression of floundering in their careers have been characterized as following a *variant* career pattern: 6 percent of our group fall into this pattern.

A respondent whose career is classified as variant started as a public health nurse. After taking her graduate degree in health education she became a health educator for a state tuberculosis association. Her marriage to a forest ranger-naturalist prevented her from continuing in this field. She found her subsequent jobs where there was a demand for female labor in isolated communities—telephone operator, typist, self-employed nursery school director. At present she is teaching in a nursery school attached to a church. Her "career" shows little direction or progression.

Another woman with a variant pattern received a Ph.D. in fine arts in 1957. She had spent the previous ten years performing various editorial chores for a publisher. She intended to work in the field of psychology of art after securing her degree but she was unable to find employment. She has continued to do proofreading and clerical work except for occasional brief consultations in her field. At present she is a part-time proofreader for a national magazine.

This brings us to the last category—those who had no career patterns, not even a variant one, because they had worked for less than three years. Twelve percent fall into this category. A woman who earned her undergraduate degree in 1945 and an M.A. in 1946 worked for less than three years as an industrial chemist. She then left the labor force to get married and remained at home bringing up her two children. She did not return to work until 1963. At this point we classify her as having no career pattern, although now that she is back at work she may develop one.

Another respondent without a career pattern is a young woman who received her B.A. in 1946 and her master's degree in social work the following year. She worked for two years and then quit at the time her first child was born. When her youngster was four she took a part-time job for a few months, but shortly thereafter left again because of pregnancy. Since then she has worked for only a part of one year, substituting for the director of a nursery school.

When we exclude the 35 women who had no career pattern, we find the interrelations between career patterns and the work histories of the remaining 276 shown in Table 6.12. We see that those who had continuous work histories were most likely to have a broad career pattern. This is not surprising since it requires time and substantial continuity of work experience to move away from a narrow field and at the same time to improve one's position. More women with a broken work history followed a changed career pattern than any other. Apparently those who withdrew several times from the labor force either changed their minds

TABLE 6.12

Career Pattern	*Work History* continuous	broken	terminated
Straight	24	27	46
Broad	43	28	26
Changed	28	33	21
Variant	5	12	7
Total (N = 276)	*100*	*100*	*100*

about what they wanted to do or could not find work in their chosen fields.

If we juxtapose marital status and career pattern, we find that single women were most likely to be in the broad or changed categories and that married women without children were most likely to follow a broad pattern. Both of these subgroups had much more freedom to branch out or to change their occupational objectives. In this connection, we should recall the earlier findings about the impact of large families on work history. Those with three or more children were not likely to work continuously and were therefore unlikely to have a broad or changed career pattern, if any.

The fact that only 11 percent of the group had no careers and only another 6 percent had variant ones underscores once again the significant role that purposeful and directed work plays in the lives of these young women. Despite the many changing circumstances and conditions to which they had to respond and adjust, the important fact is that most of them sought and succeeded in developing a career.

The burden of the foregoing materials now is clear. The preceding chapter stressed that home and volunteer activities do not engage the full interest and energy of most of the women in our group. This chapter has helped to clarify the extent to which they sought meaningful places for themselves in the world of work. Most pursued careers, some have settled for jobs. But most important only 34 out of 311, or 11 percent, had little or no connection to the labor market. The rest had fairly strong connections—about half have had continuous employment. In short, most of these women have a mind to work.

7

Occupational Achievement

Most people who work are concerned with the income they earn, the responsibility they are able to exercise on their jobs, and other rewards for performance. To broaden our understanding of the role of work in the lives of educated women, we must study and assess their occupational achievement.

Despite the opportunities that have been opened up for women in recent decades, the occupational structure is still heavily differentiated according to sex. There are fields in which men account overwhelmingly for the proportion of workers, such as corporate and engineering management, and there are other fields where women predominate, such as nursing, library science, and social work.

There is another distinction based on sex that has particular relevance to the present analysis. Leadership positions in most fields are largely filled by men. While there are many reasons for this, the fact remains that sex discrimination plays an important role. It is harder for a woman to be appointed or promoted to a leadership position than it is for a man. Men continue to hold the vast majority of top positions and they continue to favor their own sex. The world of work still belongs primarily, if no longer exclusively, to men.

Every large organization is hierarchically structured, so there are only a limited number of good jobs at the top. Those most likely to obtain one of these better paying, more desirable positions are individuals who have acquired superior education and training and have demonstrated superior skill and competence. Each of these qualifications is a result of time, effort, and perseverance. Our group of intelligent and well-educated women were in a good position to compete in the job market. And they were able to make changes in their career plans if they found that, for one reason or another, they did not want to continue in the fields for which they had originally trained.

But once they began to work, they were no longer so flexible. We know from the materials that have already been reviewed that many married women, particularly those with several children, must cope with major responsibilities both at home and on the job and divide their time and energy accordingly. This makes it difficult for them to compete with men who can direct almost all of their energies to accomplishing their career goals.

Moreover, the women in our group did not have to earn enough from their work to support themselves and others. Young men know that they will have to be breadwinners for their families. A few women among our single group apparently had to assume some responsibility for their parents. And a few married women who had lost their husbands by death or divorce had to support themselves and their children. However, most of the women in our group did not have the financial spur to maximize their occupational accomplishments that pushes most men. Even those who attached the greatest importance to working did not necessarily, or even usually, direct their lives toward climbing up to the highest rung on the occupational ladder. The social status of a married women is usually, in the first instance, a function not of her own accomplishments, but of those of her husband. It is his position and his income which determine her place in the social hierarchy. While some women in our group, particularly the single women, looked to their jobs as their primary source of status and satisfaction, this was not true of most of them.

A key measure of an individual's occupational achievement in a competitive society is the amount of money that he earns. Table 7.1 sets forth the earnings of the 226

TABLE 7.1

Present Salary	*Percent*
less than $2,500	6
$2501–$5000	7
$5001–$7500	20
$7501–$10,000	24
$10,001–$12,500	15
$12,501–$15,000	8
$15,001–$20,000	4
$20,001+	2
no salary	4
not known	10
Total	*100*

women who were employed at the time they replied to our questionnaire. Because most of these women, being young, are still some distance from their maximum earning power, because many of them have had to drop out of work for some period of time, and because many were working part time because of their responsibilities at home, the fact that almost 1 out of every 3 earns $10,000 or more is noteworthy.

While the salary that an individual earns is often the best single index of the level of his occupational achievement, it is not the only one that can be used. In some cases, as with members of religious orders, it cannot be used at all. To refine our measures of occupational achievement, we also took into account the rank which our women held, the quality of the institutions which employed them, and the degree of responsibility attached to their jobs.

In establishing cut-off points for a fourfold category scheme consisting of high, good, fair, and low achievement levels, we took into account differences in salary levels in various types of employing institutions, such as government and business and differences in prestige of employing institutions. For example, a full professorship at a small teachers' college has less prestige than an associate professorship at a major university. Furthermore, different vocations command different rewards. A successful librarian rarely receives the same salary as a successful lawyer.

We did not encounter any particular difficulties in classifying the respondents in either of the two top achievement levels. Those who were on neither of these levels were placed in the "fair" category if they were making use of their educational background and training. Those who were working at a level below that which their education and skills would indicate were placed in the "low" category. We classified only those presently working.

Following are brief descriptions of individuals on the various achievement levels. Among those on the highest level are a director of research for a mental health board in a metropolitan center with an annual salary of $15,000; an associate professor of medicine at a high-ranking medical school whose salary is $18,000; and a woman, earning far less than these two, who is the supervisor of the children's department of a large public library system.

The following are on the "good" level: a special assistant to the attorney general of a western state who receives $8 per hour for twenty to thirty hours weekly, supplementing a newly established private law practice; the bureau chief of a large county welfare department with a monthly salary of $846; an epidemiologist for a state department of public health, earning $12,000.

TABLE 7.2

Achievement Level	*Percent*
High	17
Good	31
Fair	35
Low	17
Total	*100*

The "fair" category includes: a self-employed clinical psychologist who earns around $9,500 annually; a caseworker for a child care clinic who works twenty-four hours weekly for $5 per hour; a lawyer who works about ten hours weekly as a consultant.

In the "low" category are an economist who helps her husband in his practice of optometry; a Ph.D. who works as a proofreader for a national magazine for twenty hours a week at $3 per hour; and a piano teacher who gives a few lessons at home for $4 an hour.

Table 7.2 summarizes the results of our classification of the 226 women who are working. The other 85 were not working at the time they answered our questionnaire. That almost half of the women employed fall into one of the two highest achievement levels shows that a large proportion have been able to build successfully on their education and training. On the other hand, it is equally significant that so many fall below these levels. We will therefore investigate the factors accounting for the differences.

The better one's preparation, the greater her chance for success. Moreover, those who have the desire and the perseverance to acquire a doctorate, by that alone, indicate a high degree of career interest and motivation. Table 7.3

TABLE 7.3

	Degree (in percent)	
Achievement Level	*doctorate*	*less than doctorate*
High	30	8
Good	44	21
Medium	24	44
Low	2	27
Total (N = 226)	*100*	*100*

shows a significant relation between education and achievement level. Those who had acquired a doctorate were much more likely to be in one of the higher achievement levels than those with less education.

Let us now consider whether a woman's work history is related to her achievement level. This is indicated in Table

TABLE 7.4

	Work History (in percent)	
Achievement Level	*continuous*	*broken*
High	23	7
Good	41	10
Medium	29	47
Low	7	36
Total (N = 226)	*100*	*100*

7.4. We can see that a continuous work history is almost a prerequisite for high, or even good, achievement. A woman cannot reach the top in her field unless she is willing to devote a major portion of her life to work. Continuity is a necessary factor but not, of course, the only factor. We must look for others in differential achievement.

Those in the independent professions of medicine or the law as well as those who specialized in the natural sciences tend to be at the top achievement level. This reflects, among other things, the differentially high earnings characteristic of these fields and the broadening opportunities that these women encountered because of shortages of well-trained persons in these fields.

Table 7.5 is particularly interesting; it relates career patterns and achievement levels. There is a marked consistency in these relations. More of those who followed a broad career pattern are in the top achievement levels. This group is followed by those with a straight pattern, then by those with a changed pattern, and lastly by those with a variant pattern. Equally striking is the fact that despite the loss of time and preparation involved in changing their fields of work, over a third of those with a changed pattern were at the upper end of the achievement scale.

TABLE 7.5

	Career Pattern (in percent)			
Achievement Level	*straight*	*broad*	*changed*	*variant*
High	16	27	11	0
Good	33	38	27	14
Medium	42	23	52	7
Low	9	12	10	79
Total (N = 226)	*100*	*100*	*100*	*100*

We learned earlier that the woman's family situation often conditions involvement in work. Table 7.6 considers the relationship between her family situation and her level of achievement. We find that those who are single or married without children are much more likely to have made a success of their careers. But it is worth noting that more than 40 percent of those with children were in one of the two top achievement levels. The table supports our previous conclusion that a woman's success at work will be significantly influenced by the size of her family, but this factor alone does not determine the results.

TABLE 7.6

Achievement Level	*Family Situation (in percent)*				
	single	*married, no children*	*one child*	*two children*	*three or more children*
High	24	23	12	8	11
Good	39	37	29	31	6
Medium	30	37	38	40	40
Low	7	3	21	21	43
Total (N = 226)	*100*	*100*	*100*	*100*	*100*

What a woman can accomplish in her career depends not only on her ability and the extent to which her family circumstances support or inhibit her career, but also on the attitudes and actions of those who determine personnel policy. Our questionnaire asked whether our respondents had encountered discrimination in employment. We also inquired whether their sex had ever proved to be an asset. A considerable proportion wrote that they had experienced discrimination at one time or another. This was true of women in every sector—in business, nonprofit institutions, and government.

A woman with long work experience in public health

reported: "Women are not generally promoted to high-echelon positions in public health. I have just lost a position and salary raise to a man who has less qualifications. I was told I was eligible but a man would be brought from out of state. This is not new to me." Another respondent working in the same field, with voluntary health organizations said: "If I were a man I probably would have been the executive of at least one agency." A Far Eastern expert with journalistic and government experience wrote: "My experience with prospective employers involves their giving my lengthy job experience a cursory glance, then anxiously asking, 'But can you type?' "

A field such as publishing which attracts many women is nevertheless characterized by discrimination, according to one who advanced quite far: "It is very difficult for a woman in publishing. Rarely does she attain a directorship. I have found a tendency to exploit a woman, to work her twenty-four hours a day, and to keep her in the background." In the allied field of journalism another said that "any *close* competition is still between the exceptional woman and the average man."

A woman who had been trained in international affairs and who had diversified work experience had a blanket condemnation of prevailing personnel practices: "I feel I met with prejudice in every personnel officer who interviewed me in the Department of State or later in large industrial corporations. Many of them frankly admitted to me they felt that women have no place in big business or in big jobs." Another former government employee mentioned a more subtle difficulty. "I felt my sex a definite obstacle . . . in my work in the U.S. government because the particular fields and agencies in which I was most interested (e.g., fiscal policy and international finance) were definitely dominated by men (in contrast to such fields as labor, welfare, etc.) and very few women attained high positions in the agencies in which I worked. In fact, I would say *no* women did."

A Ph.D. economist who works for a leading oil company reported that it "would not allow women economists to make formal reports to directors. All had to be relayed through a man." Even academic life is not free of prejudices. Witness this report from one of the respondents: "When I finished my Ph.D. in musicology at ——— I would have loved to go on and teach there as many of my male fellow-students subsequently did. I was told I couldn't because I was a woman." It all seemed very clear to one woman who wrote that "being a woman is a deficiency similar to being colored, pock-marked, or lame." Another pointed out that "a professional *woman* lacks the assistance of a *wife*."

It is clear that many of our women believed they were handicapped in the pursuit of their careers because of their sex. Another group, however, believed that being a woman did not hinder their progress. A former employee of the U.S. Department of Interior wrote: "My employers in Washington had one thing in common—they hired and promoted solely on the basis of ability, not because of sex. For them, the battle over women's rights was over. This undoubtedly eased the way for me."

In a quite different field, science, a professor of biology wrote: "Most of my male acquaintances—teachers, fellow students, colleagues—have expressed doubts about women in science, giving various general and broad . . . reasons for their attitudes; in practice, however, they have all too often been more helpful to me than to each other."

The same feeling of lessened competition between men

and women was reported by an art historian: "There is a genuine advantage to academic women in the fact that they are not taken seriously enough to arouse jealousy and so their ideas are more readily accepted than those of male colleagues."

Others pointed to the advantage that accrues to a minority group. A lawyer wrote: "When a woman does a good job on a particular project, it is more likely to be remembered and credited to her than the same job would be to a man very frequently." In this she was seconded by a psychiatrist who remarked: "As a matter of fact, it is easier to get notice as a woman."

TABLE 7.7

Experience Reported		*Percent*
Encountered discrimination		40
obstacles only	33	
obstacles and assistance	7	
Did not encounter discrimination		60
found assistance	7	
neither obstacles nor assistance	53	
Total		*100*

Several commented on how helpful their employers had been, especially those whose wives work. A biologist reported that her employer had "a conscious desire to show that a woman could have a family *and* a successful scientific career. His willingness to accept my leaves of absence and part-time work made all the difference to me."

Although these comments are suggestive, we were not able to discern any consistent pattern with respect to sex discrimination. As Table 7.7 indicates, the majority of the group did not report any obstacles and only 1 out of 3 reported obstacles only.

Table 7.8 shows how those who reported that they had encountered obstacles specified them.

We found no significant relationship between the discrimination or assistance that women encountered in employment and their achievement level. This reflects the fact that only 47 percent of the entire group reported experiencing either discrimination or assistance.

We have uncovered a number of significant relationships between the level of occupational achievement of our women and other facets of their lives, particularly their education, fields of specialization, career patterns, and family structure. The overriding determinant was unquestionably the number of years spent at work. Those who had a more or less continuous work history were much more likely to do well while those who had only a brief or intermittent work pattern had little opportunity to secure or hold a preferred position.

TABLE 7.8

Nature of Obstacle	*Percent*
Hiring	41
Assignment	13
Pay	16
Promotion	30
Total	*100*

How can we evaluate the achievement of these women? That almost half are in the top two levels seems striking, but it also means that over half have not had a successful career. This primarily reflects their limited time in the labor force. Faced with a choice between family and career, many decided to seek a balance between them rather than to pursue their occupational goals to the exclusion of others. The women give every indication that they will increase their work participation as their children grow older, and the resumption of full-time work will undoubtedly result in a rise in their achievement levels.

8

Accommodation

We have described the options of the educated woman with respect to different facets of her life. We have seen that these concern primarily education, marriage, children, work, and volunteer activities. Whatever options a woman exercises, she finds in the course of time that she must continually accommodate to new situations. In this chapter, we shall describe situations that forced modifications in the plans of the women in our group, and the means by which they accommodated to the new situations.

All of these women agreed on one decision—to pursue graduate education. However, for some, the choice of field of study was determined by their anticipations about the future and was selected on the basis of compatibility with family life or ease of reentry into the labor market after interruption of work. One respondent wrote: "I knew I would stop work when I had children—accounting seemed to be a career that might be picked up again at a later date." Another recalled: "At age twenty-one, I thought that medicine would be too demanding for compatible union with marriage and family. Social casework appeared to be a profession that could be combined with marriage and a family with minimum of complaint." Another: "My field of home economics is a good one for a woman—I don't have to compete with men to achieve . . . and my husband considers it a feminine role so that somehow there isn't much competition there."

The length of their education varied with their choice of field and with their commitment to education and to a career. Some were in fields that had fairly specific short-term requirements, and others had the option of continuing their education to the Ph.D. or of stopping before attaining a doctorate. Many pursued their education with intensity, and were willing to forego other options either temporarily or permanently in its favor.

One woman wrote: "I know that the higher I go on the educational ladder, the less are my chances for marriage. It is working out as expected. Of course, I'm still studying." A professor of English said: "I was aware that having a Ph.D. would narrow the field with regard to marriage. If I married, it would have to be to a man who approved of, and encouraged, a professional wife." Another professor of English wrote about the same problem: "The higher you go academically, the harder it is to find a suitable husband because (a) you are fussier and (b) American men are scared of educated women." And one said: "As a Negro woman, I was aware that this decreased the number of Negro men who would feel secure as a life mate with a girl holding a Ph.D."

Despite their misgivings, each of these four women went on to earn a doctorate. Others faced with specific alternate opportunities, such as marriage or work, accommodated to these new options by ending their graduate studies. One woman deliberately did not complete her Ph.D.: "I felt it would be a serious disadvantage in regard to marriage." Another did not pursue her first preference to study medicine. "If I had been a man, I would have borrowed and gone anyway. As a woman, I did not want such a high debt to pay back, lest I not work long enough." Another said: "I could have finished my Ph.D. at Columbia and made a career of economics. I did not want a Ph.D.—felt it might burden my marriage." According to one woman: "A professor pooh-poohed my 'book-larnin' and sent me out into the world at a time when I would otherwise have gone on for the Ph.D."

A government official reported: "I planned to pursue the doctorate and then—just maybe—consider marriage. Having progressed so far in my career, while many of the eligibles were away at war, I was rather busy and comfortable in what I was doing. When I was married—at forty—only the dissertation stood between me and the doctor's degree and it still stands there even though I expect to finish it."

We see that some women felt that they placed their marital prospects in jeopardy by prolonging their education. Others made definite decisions to remain unmarried or to postpone marriage as part of the basic strategy of their lives. There is the librarian who reacted against her parents' attitude "that women should marry and men work. This convinced me that a career was infinitely preferable!" Another shied away from marriage later on. "I heard my fellow classmates who were married discuss their problems. I think I decided then that society would be my husband and children." A professor of chemistry wrote: "I did not feel then, and do not now, that I could combine marriage and a career and accomplish all I wanted to in my field." A professor of art put it bluntly: "Decided one cannot serve two masters well."

A Ph.D. psychologist said that she remained single because: "I felt that I would grow restless in marriage, might push my husband to accomplish more than he wished to achieve or towards goals of my own, and that most men would find my intense and varied interests hard to live with." Another respondent wrote: "I was aware that foreign service is, for a woman, incompatible with marriage. As I did not wish to marry until at least thirty, the only thing required was not to be carried away by the glamour of the job. Eventually, I set my sights on teaching, which is not incompatible, depending on the man." She married at the age of thirty-two.

Of course, many women who remained single did not purposefully decide not to marry. They did not find acceptable marriage partners, and they have had to make adjustments in light of this unfulfilled goal. "I was sure I wanted to marry and felt I wanted to choose someone who could share my interests and whose interests I could share. I felt that I could not give up a career in order to marry. I was equally certain that I did not wish to engage in career rivalry, nor to dominate the career of a husband any more than I wished to be dominated. I have not married, but I feel my personal relationships with men in the profession have beeen facilitated by some of these expectations and anticipated problems."

Once a woman marries, her husband's attitude and his career often elicit various types of accommodation. Some women in our group ended their education when they married, while others, with the cooperation of their husbands, were able to continue. "I studied five years toward my

Ph.D. in Romance languages, completed all courses, and passed my prelims. One week later, I married an Air Force officer and have not continued my dissertation since." Said another: "Marriage directed my attention toward aiding my husband attain his graduate degree instead of getting my Ph.D." Also: "My husband obtained the Ph.D. and left Columbia for postgraduate work after three years of my graduate work had been completed. Of course I went with him."

On the other hand, a medical research worker told us: "My husband and I undertook the same graduate training at the same time and we felt it added to a marriage to be trained and instructed in similar subjects. We realized that some change in my career plans would have to be made later to allow for children which we both wanted." Another respondent wrote: "My husband and I decided even before our marriage that I should continue working on my Ph.D. and teaching. We also agreed that we'd like to start a family at least by the time I was thirty. We held to these decisions."

A husband's income can serve either to help or to hinder his wife's plans. It may be large enough to defray any costs incurred by her working or to permit her to stay home if she wishes. On the other hand, the husband's financial situation may even force a wife to earn a supplementary income, or may be such that he cannot afford the household and other costs not covered by the salary of a working wife.

A language instructor in one of the Seven Sister colleges reported: "My husband's income made it possible for me to work at a time when I made less than any help we hired. Without that, I couldn't have afforded to work." Another, a college teacher married to a scientist, told us: "My husband has always supported me so that I could work at part-time teaching instead of working for money."

A homemaker said of her husband: "He is now doing well enough that I need not resume a career for financial reasons." Another stated: "I do not have the drive to work, probably because it would not really pay, as taxes would take most of my earnings." And a college teacher reported that the "standard of living to which we aspire has directly influenced my working." For a sociologist, "the beginning of a writing career for my husband meant no income. At that point I went to work to help out. We think of it as a joint procedure."

Aside from financial considerations a husband's career can have either salutary or obstructive effects on his wife's work. Similarity of field not only adds to their common interest but may permit her to work with him, either as a partner or as an aide. Even if a wife decides to forego her career temporarily, if her husband's career is in the same area she can remain abreast of developments in the field and thus ease her reentry into the labor market.

A geologist reported: "The jobs I have had since marriage have been held jointly or cooperatively with my husband." An anthropologist commented that she collaborates with her husband in "our field work." A social scientist said: "My husband and I have the same vocation, with the result that we can share, in addition to everything else, our professional interests. This sharing has added something very beautiful to our marriage." A lawyer reported: "Since my husband is also an attorney and many years of my practice have been in partnership with him, his attitudes have markedly assisted my pursuit of my professional career. He has given me enthusiastic support in my professional activities . . . and has always considered my work as important as his." A former chemistry student found that "through my husband's work, I have kept thinking about chemical problems, see more chemical journals than I would otherwise, and talk more chemistry." Much the same was reported by a social worker. "My husband helps tremendously since he is in the same field; our common interest helps us and makes our home life livelier, I am sure. I'll continue to read his professional magazines and he'll prod me every now and then about getting out and doing something about an area of my concern."

However, being in the same field as her husband may present difficulties for a woman. She may have reservations about having a career similar to her husband's or, more often, she finds that departmental policies restrict her opportunities to work. A lawyer stopped working because of a "desire not to compete with my husband in the same profession." A social scientist remarked that she had only a "slim chance of permanent appointment at the university because my husband is in the same field—rules against nepotism apply informally here." A similar comment was made by another woman in the same area: "Since my husband and I want to teach in college and many colleges have rules against employment of husband and wife, we are very restricted as to location." A scientist reported that while her husband and she had worked on three jobs together, "our employers profited rather than lost by this arrangement." She recognizes the reluctance of many employers to hire man and wife and is considering shifting her area of concentration in order to avoid this difficulty.

Since in most marriages a husband's career is the primary

one, it can inhibit his wife's work when the location of his work limits her opportunities. A Ph.D. scientist reported: "I left a field of research . . . in which I was gaining some small reputation as a result of publications to be married and move to ———. The position I accepted in ——— was not in the same field and did not advance my career." A former teacher reported that she had "drifted into industrial jobs of secretarial and personnel nature because my husband moved about quite a lot and I could not find teaching jobs . . . as quickly as industrial jobs."

An anatomist who had the rank of assistant professor at a major medical school had to resign when her husband joined a medical group in a locality beyond commuting distance. She reported, "I have *no* plans for the immediate future. . . . If there is an opportunity to pursue my career there, either immediately or in a few years, I would like to do so. However, I may find it impractical from the point of view of commuting, baby-sitters, etc." A professor of medicine said: "I am unable to leave this area because of my husband's work, although better job opportunities may be available elsewhere."

When her husband's career has a limiting effect upon a woman's career, she may make modifications in her original aspirations. An economist remarked that her "knowledge of economics and finance has enabled me to help my husband. I keep his books, prepare tax returns, and 'enjoy' the stock market with him." Another wife said: "Since my marriage I consider being the wife of a college professor as my primary career and I do not think I could fulfill this career if I continued as a full-time college teacher myself. This meant of course that as a teacher I cannot look forward to advancements or the rewards, e.g., myself being a professor, which I once envisaged, but I have absolutely no regrets. . . . I could obtain full-time work as a college teacher only by taking a job at least thirty or forty miles from our home."

Of course motherhood places restrictions upon a woman's ability to work, and some married women, knowing this, give their careers priority and decide not to have children. A lawyer who married a colleague wrote: "I have a husband who agrees with my goals and who considers both of our careers more important than having children."

Other women postponed having children in order to enter into or continue their careers. "Full-time study and a full-time job caused me to postpone having children with resulting guilt." Another member of the group reported: "Our combined income was what deferred children and required me to work until my husband's degree was completed." In another instance children were postponed until the woman was set on her career, "until I completed graduate work and made a start on a job."

Some women who wish to have children but find they are unable to do so continue careers that they might have otherwise interrupted. A childless economist who has worked continuously said: "I envisioned staying home with my children until they were about four years old so that I could myself influence their early development."

The number of children a woman has, as we have shown, exerts a major influence on her later options. Consequently, a woman may decide to limit the size of her family in order to continue working or to finish her education. A scientist said: "I'm sure I would have tried to have another child if doing so had not meant that a new Ph. D. would have to be put on ice."

A mother's decision to work (or study) is affected by a number of factors. First, there is her evaluation of her children's needs and how they can best be satisfied. Some mothers believe that their children require their full-time attention and they therefore retire from or cut down on work for varying periods, depending on their estimates of the length of time their children need them.

An historian summarized her life as mother of three: "My children's needs stopped my work on the Ph.D. from 1957 to 1961. I have always felt able to do any two of study, teach, run my home, but never all three. As there's been no question about the children, the other two have taken turns." Another who had not yet acquired a doctorate in the sciences pointed out: "It has been impossible with small children to take course work or do home study to remedy the background." One mother admitted: "I do not feel very comfortable being out of the house more than one to two days with a pre-school child at home." Another, who is expecting her first child, stated: "I do not expect to work full time for five or six years."

More than one woman found that her efforts to do everything—and to do it well—just exceeded her capacity: "I did not have the physical strength to meet the demands of home, husband, young children, and job. I did not earn enough money to compensate for the effort. The children (then two and four years old) were not happy in nursery school ten hours a day." She resigned from her job.

Others learned that their children's needs change: "I was amazed to find that as my children got older, they seemed to need more of my time. I sometimes help them with school work, must transport them around town for music lessons, Hebrew school (three times a week), and so on."

A mother of four wrote: "The five years of part-time teaching that I did were done during the period when my first three children were all very young. During the hours I was away they required mostly physical care and that I could find in excellent quality. Now that three of them are teen-agers (or close to it) I would hesitate very much about undertaking a job which would require me to be away when they arrived home from school. . . . The problems of the teen-ager are immediate ones—unless met when they occur, they may never be met at all."

Other women are less committed to the proposition that motherhood means retirement from work and believe that both their needs and their children's are best met if they work full time. "Friends' advice, especially the type urging me to 'quit work and stay home with the children,' flows off my back like water off a duck's. *I would not be content to be Just a Housewife*." A scientist: "I am now working full time instead of two days a week. The children are older and need to learn to take care of themselves."

A journalist said: "If they were being insecure, I would quit, but prejudiced as I am, I think they are among the best-behaved kids I know." A social worker, mother of three, realized that her working "created some conflicts but was a most rewarding course. Perhaps my eldest son suffered most from my conflicted feeling, as I spent most time with him but resented it most." But she appreciated that "like all civilizing influences, work increases the complexity of life and the depth of its interest."

The attitudes of the fathers are of major importance. Those who accept their wives' work frequently reinforce their approval by assisting in household chores and otherwise easing the way. The husband of a woman with a

Ph.D. and two children "encouraged me not to abandon teaching altogether: he has arranged for enough domestic help to make it just possible for me to carry on. When I have been discouraged . . . he has helped me to be patient." A social worker with two children preferred a psychological interpretation: "Husband (a salesman) feels my working is my choice—it is no threat to him." And a Ph.D. scientist reported that since "my mother-in-law has always worked . . . my husband expected me to be interested in a career."

A librarian with two children reported: "My husband's attitudes are ideal for my working. He is proud of my accomplishments, very helpful at home, and sympathetic when I'm tired." Much the same supportive attitude was reported by a mother of four who was able to return to teaching as her children grew up because of "my husband's encouragement and willingness to put up with a less-than-perfect household."

When children are of school age, their mother's ability to work may depend on whether their father and they are willing to assume some responsibility for the household chores. A mother of three who is now studying full time and who has worked intermittently said of her husband: "He is 'extraordinary' . . . he has helped me in every possible way, coming home if a child was sick and I couldn't, overlooking sloppy housekeeping and casual cooking, etc." The working mother of six, a scientist, said about her children: "They take my working as a matter-of-fact thing and pitch in on housework, washing dishes, cooking, baby care, etc." Another, a mother of three, whose work involves her in some out-of-town meetings, reported that "the girls run the house for a couple of days."

In several instances husbands took the initiative to get their wives out of the home into a job. A mother of four wrote: "My husband has always urged me to work. He would like to see me do so again." A sociologist, divorced from a psychiatrist, said: "My husband insisted upon my going back to school after we married and getting my Ph.D. degree." She added: "I would have preferred to stay home with my child but my husband's wishes made that impossible." A journalist who worked continuously said that her lawyer husband "is proud of my position and believes my outside contacts make me a more interesting wife. Naturally, I am interested in pleasing him."

A psychologist married to a physicist described her husband's attitudes about her working as "dual." "If I had taken a job which was beneath my educational level he would have disapproved of my taking time away from the children and himself, too. Since I have a job full of creative opportunities . . . he has made it a point to do more things with and for the children to ease their adjustment to my being away part of the time now." A physician's report contained the following note added by her dentist husband: "The major problem with which intelligent and educated women must contend is vain and pretentious men."

When a husband disapproves of his wife's working, this can be a prime factor in a wife's decision to remain at home. A woman with three children who had earned the Ph.D. in the humanities reported that her husband "disliked my writing attempts, has never shown any interest in reading even what has been published." However, she added, his opposition was less intense when she held a teaching position.

Another reported that her psychiatrist husband would

"flip" if she didn't stay home with her young children. The wife of a utility president indicated his limited approval of her working: "If it's ladylike and can be done during the day while he's at the office—O.K.!" A mother of four who used to teach explained: "I have had to restrict myself to part-time activities and study when my husband is busy . . . because he dislikes my infringement on 'his time.'" A former college teacher with two children perceived that her working seems to "create family tensions and make it difficult for my husband to perform at his peak level."

The wife of another business executive, mother of two children, said that her husband "never wanted me to work outside, but I am free to participate in any other activities as time and inclination allow." She had pursued graduate studies in social work, but she found it possible to meet her husband's preference by changing to piano-teaching at home. One social worker wrote: "My husband's devotion to his career has involved a certain unwillingness (which he would deny) to relieve me of some houseworking responsibilities."

Another, a mother of three, married to an academician, explained why she could not pursue her career: "My husband would not be willing nor does he have the time to 'baby-sit' or help with household chores so that I could work or study." A physician with two children, looking back on her unhappy marriage which ended in divorce, concluded: "Most of the difficulties might have been avoided if I had chosen a more sympathetic partner. As it was, my former husband became progressively more and more opposed to my having a career."

Even when a mother wishes to work and her husband approves, she must make arrangements for the care of her children while she is away from home. For some women, the presence of a relative in the home lightens her child-rearing burdens. Others must seek paid domestic help and the availability, cost, and competence of such assistance affects a mother's work decisions. Those who have been able to hire competent domestic help have been able to further their career ambitions while, for others who cannot do so, work is usually impossible.

One professional woman reported: "My mother has lived with us since the birth of our first child . . . I don't do much child care . . . my mother enjoys it and is more than willing to assume the major part of it." A lawyer who recently returned to a twenty-five-hour-a-week work schedule explained that "this was possible by assistance of my mother-in-law who cared for my infant when I was employed the first year and a half after his birth and is presently made possible because my mother-in-law comes to take care of my house while I am at work and is here during the children's vacations and days off from school." A psychiatrist who found it difficult to secure competent help when her children were small reported that when her mother-in-law came to live with her "this increased my freedom." The extended family may be a rarity, but a female relative who lives in the home is still to be found.

A lawyer who has had a continuous working pattern explained: "My decision to pursue my profession was never influenced by such factors (cost of help, taxes, etc.). My decision was made first and the attendant problems met when they arose. The only factor which would have altered my decision would have been unavailability of competent help for my children." Another reported: "I have been extremely fortunate in having the same exceedingly competent housekeeper for seven years."

A college teacher who has worked continuously remarked: "A working mother is completely dependent on help." A part-time college teacher said, "Perhaps if household assistance were cheaper I would have worked full time." Another woman stated: "The cost, unreliability, and unavailability of really good help has influenced me not to depend on a regular substitute for me in the home."

The question of competence is, of course, subjective, and many women believe that few, if any, mother substitutes are capable of taking their place. "If there were such a thing as a real mother substitute that money could buy, I might work while my children are pre-school. But there ain't no such animal—the kids need me!!" Much the same viewpoint was set forth by a woman who had had a long work history but who stayed home when her children were young: "So often the joker in the deck is the person who substitutes at home for the mother. There is no one: the joint family doesn't exist. The maiden aunt has an apartment (and a life) of her own. The grandmother is not wanted."

Other work decisions frequently occasioned by the presence of children involve the scheduling of work time. Some mothers with domestic help, cooperative husbands, and a strong career drive, are able to work continuously. Others accommodate to family's needs by working less than full time or on schedules adapted to those of their husband and children. "I am one of the lucky ones because next week I plan to start a part-time job doing economic research. I shall work two days a week. . . . I can take the job even though my younger child is only three because it is only two days a week and I already have help on those days and further I am not required to be at the office at a particularly early hour."

A lawyer who recently became town clerk wrote: "I did not wish full-time work since my children are still quite young. . . . This opening unexpectedly arose in the village where I live, and though I was not planning to return to work, the circumstances seemed ideal." A social worker with a history of full-time employment is looking forward to less than a full-time job "so that the household chores won't be additional and all week-end activities." And a physicist reported that "working part time lets one have one's cake and eat it too—but you have to compromise your ambitions."

A social scientist shifted from research to teaching "as a result of marriage and childbearing. . . . I can't do research on a part-time basis and feel adequate—teaching is an easier combination with early stages of family." Several others also reported that teaching is easier to dovetail with child-rearing responsibilities than most alternative types of employment. One woman who shifted from social work to teaching wrote: "Teaching gave me a work schedule which permitted me to be at home when my children were not in school." Several women reported that they looked on school teaching not as a career but as a job and would prefer teaching at the collegiate level but could not spare the time from their families, that an academic position demanded. However, a woman who had held a college position continuously except for one year found considerable flexibility in her work and "wouldn't consider another type of job."

A few respondents were able to work out what they considered ideal arrangements. An economist, working on a contract basis for a large research organization, said that this left her "complete freedom as to how many hours and which hours to work and also minimizes the difficulties of adaptation to changes in location of husband's work. This has meant . . . no necessity to stop work for birth of child . . . just reduce amount of work."

Since few employers can permit such a flexible arrangement, working at home presented more of a challenge to other women although some ventured the attempt. A writer reported that she had "decided two years ago to attempt a free-lance career at home, as supplement to husband's income and to continue my own interests in writing but without full-time job." Another, a Ph.D. scientist, wrote: "My duties at home are such as to allow me only evening hours for work. This meant primarily literature work rather than laboratory research. This position would make it possible for me to keep in touch with the progress in biochemistry." A lawyer reported, "Self-employment enables me to arrange for time with my children when necessary or desirable."

The dovetailing of vacations represented another challenge. We have already noted that teaching is attractive because mothers are free when their children are out of school. One respondent, whose husband is a music teacher who travels during the summer, shifted from social work to teaching so that their schedules would dovetail.

Some mothers make modifications in their original career goals in order to better cope with their maternal responsibilities. A mother of two summarized her situation as follows: "In work such as mine (biological research) there is no use denying that a married woman with children is at a distinct disadvantage . . . I have been able to manage successfully only by recognizing that I could not expect to work anywhere near my full potential." A psychologist reflected on her experiences: "I'm sorry I haven't the Ph.D. But if I can end up doing some good research without it—or teaching perhaps (though this seems doubtful given the *rigid* insistence on Ph.D. now at universities) I shall be very happy. . . . If these past ten years as homemaker have meant I shall never be 'famous' so I'll never be 'famous'!"

Others lowered their achievement goals as a method of accommodating to the increased demands of marriage and family; a physician with a university appointment wrote, "I have definitely modified my aspirations and cut down working hours because it was apparent that my children were not getting proper love and care when I worked full time." A part time instructor in Russian said: "So far, since my children are quite young, I feel that I should limit my vocational goals . . . I am interested in using my educational background, at least while my children are young, in a *limited* way only."

Some mothers have accommodated by interrupting their careers while their children were young and then have either resumed their education in their former field or in a new one preliminary to a return to work, or have returned directly to work on either a part-time or a full-time basis. "I undertook work in education as soon as all of my children were in school," wrote one. "Because of my children, I developed a strong interest in education and wanted to learn more about it and contribute something. School hours, which coincided with my children's, influenced my choice."

A former teacher felt that she was helping to keep up her skills by responding to the request of her minister to undertake a voluntary nursery school survey, "a wonderful opportunity for me to use my education, teaching experience, and creative ability." Another is keeping her skills fresh by additional study, thus "preparing myself for a profession when my children grow up."

A journalist said: "My present job places me in the transitional, or part-time phase, I had planned for after my ten years at home. I feel that in another three years when my children are in school all day long, the full-time job I will look for will enable me to experience career growth." A chemist with a Ph.D. took up Russian studies "to allow me to translate chemistry articles and work at home, while taking care of the children. Later I was asked to get a teaching degree as they will need Russian teachers in the high school here." One respondent who had studied English in graduate school and who had been primarily occupied as a homemaker for fourteen years "sub-taught in the local public schools two to three days a week for a year. This year I am taking education courses toward my state teaching certification, preparatory to full-time teaching." Another mother reported: "Considering that I chose to put marriage before a career, I believe my experiences have exceeded my expectations. With three children ten or older, I have been able to accept the opportunity of part-time college teaching, and I love it."

Another wrote: "I have just started working as a research assistant in psychology at half time. The job offered to me sounded like very interesting research—a chance to get back into psychology on a professional level. Since my youngest begins kindergarten this fall, it seemed too fine an opportunity for creative work to let it slip." And another: "I had temporarily retired from law practice and after about three years out I felt some anxiety about my continuing abilities in the field, and I just missed it. So I applied to Radcliffe's Institute for Independent Study, and got a grant to do research." A research sociologist said: "I stayed out of employment while my first two children were very young, and suffered boredom and psychosomatic complaints until I returned to teaching and work."

We have seen that single and married women must make accommodations; similarly those whose marriages are broken by divorce or widowhood face new situations. If a woman has been working she need not necessarily make a change when her marriage ends unless support of children requires increased income. But if a woman had been home when her marriage ended, she may return to school or to work not only in order to support herself and her children, but also to make a new life for herself. A public health executive reported: "My graduate study was *after* marriage and divorce. I realized the necessity of a graduate degree for the kind of position I needed to have to raise and support my daughter. I have always worked to support her and myself." A government official stated that, after her divorce, "I had to rely on my own career development again for income and opportunities to spend, travel, or buy a home." A writer with three children wrote, "I had no life outside the home during my marriage. This was the reason for the divorce. Since my divorce was made final, I have engaged in an active career of writing and criticism and editing (living on alimony)."

A lawyer noted that the death of her husband "increased the work load and financial responsibilities. I am now supporting my two children and have done so for the last eleven years since the death of my husband." Another woman said, "I went back to graduate school after my first husband dropped dead. I had had a successful career in the advertising business, which I left to go around the world. I came back and decided to start from scratch with something I really wanted to do—teach history." A government researcher, widowed since 1946, said: "I had to earn my living. But the twentieth century, which made possible my education and being able to earn a good livelihood, also condemned me and single working women to a life of loneliness such as no family woman, no 'religieuse,' and no man in our society, married or unmarried, can even guess at. I call working women like me 'lay sisters.' "

Just as there were marked differences in the basic strategies that these women adopted with respect to education, marriage, and career, so their methods of coping with their responsibilities for homemaking and children reveal a diversified pattern. Part of the diversity reflects their earlier strategies but much of it can be accounted for by the varied circumstances and conditions of their lives, including in particular their husbands' careers, the availability of good household help, and the number and age of their children.

Important as these factors were, they should not mask the presence of another: the values of these women as reflected in their choices with respect to the options which they faced. Those who wanted very much to pursue a career were usually able to cope with the problems of family as well, and those who found satisfaction in homemaking and child rearing or who felt these took precedence over other concerns did not choose full-time careers.

9

Satisfactions and Fulfillment

We have identified in earlier chapters the principal sources of the gratifications and disappointments our women experienced in three major sectors of their lives—family, work, and volunteer activities. In this chapter we will determine whether these women are generally satisfied with the overall pattern of their lives. To this end, we shall examine the various sources of their gratifications, the extent to which their earlier expectations have been met, and the extent to which they wish to make changes in the future. On the basis of this analysis, we will determine the degree of success that our women have achieved in using the many options which were open to them. In this way we will have a clearer perception of whether the multiple options which these women confronted enabled them to increase their gratifications. Opportunities are a precondition for satisfaction, but they do not assure it.

In order to determine to what degree and in what ways the sources of gratification in each area were similar and in what ways they were complementary, we attempted to make the categories comparable. Table 9.1 sets forth the basic data.

Since we have previously discussed in chapters V and VI the gratifications which our women derived from home, volunteer activities, and work we will not discuss this aspect of the problem in detail here. Instead we will present a comparative analysis. We see first that as a source of gratification, personal relations loom large in each sector. This finding is consonant with conclusions of other studies, both of occupational choice and work adjustment, which have shown that women tend to be more "people-oriented" than men. This may explain, at least in part, why women predominate in such fields as teaching, nursing, and social work.

TABLE 9.1

	Home		*Work*		*Volunteer Activities*	
Source of Gratification	*no.*	*percent*	*no.*	*percent*	*no.*	*percent*
Nature of activity	117	33	119	24	22	10
Self-realization	23	7	107	22	46	19
Personal relations	155	44	127	26	72	31
Social significance	28	8	94	19	84	37
Conditions	30	8	48	9	7	3
Total	*353*	*100*	*495*	*100*	*231*	*100*

Although many of our women derived similar satisfactions from the different facets of their lives, particularly from personal relations, each area was particularly suited to provide a particular gratification. Home offers the greatest opportunity for personal relationships, paid employment is the area in which most women can achieve self-realization, volunteers found their greatest satisfaction in being of service to others.

We all know that home and family offer great opportunity for gratification through enabling women to create and maintain a constructive environment for husband and children. But only a very small minority—1 out of 14—find an opportunity at home for self-realization. This is one reason that so many of our women found it necessary and desirable to work, continuously or at least intermittently. Work offers an opportunity for the self-realization which had been part of their planning for a very long time. Work is the primary arena in which these women can find this source of gratification.

So far we have indicated the types of gratification which women are likely to derive in these major areas. However, since every human being operates simultaneously in several spheres, we cannot consider each field as if it were exclusive. Attitudes result from a composite of experiences in every area in which one has or is engaged. Moreover, while home, work, and volunteer activities comprise the fields in which a woman is likely to devote most of her time and energy, what she does in her free time is another important source of gratification. However, there is such variety in the types of pursuits in which individuals engage during their leisure that we found it impossible to deal with this aspect of their lives as systematically as with work, home, and volunteer activities.

Therefore, we developed an inclusive category scheme that would enable us to consider these women's reactions to the totality of their life circumstances. We attempted to take account also of the fact that everybody's life contains some dissatisfactions. In work, these may include commuting, red tape, long hours; at home, there are routine chores. But these are usually minor sources of discontentment and are not of transcendent importance. However, for some people, an entire realm of life, and not merely certain aspects of it, creates unhappiness. A study of the protocols disclosed that there were a number of women who were seriously dissatisfied with either their work or their personal lives.

We examined each questionnaire as a unit in order to determine what a respondent's comments, taken as a whole, indicated about her contentment with the conditions of her life. The final determination of the degree of satisfaction was derived from the pervading impression communicated by each questionnaire rather than from a formal analysis of specific responses. Several staff members reviewed each questionnaire independently in order to insure as much objectivity as possible in reaching an overall evaluation.

In our "schema of satisfaction," we put first those who seem to be satisfied with all areas of their lives. The group who are dissatisfied only with their work includes women who are unhappy about the way their work role had developed and those who have serious regrets about their inability to work. Those who are dissatisfied only with their personal lives include those who have major reservations about their role at home and those whose unhappiness stems from the lack of a home life. The fourth category consists of those who appear to be dissatisfied with both areas of their lives.

Several interesting conclusions can be derived from Table 9.2. Contrary to the common belief that educated women represent a particularly dissatisfied group, less than 1 out of 10 is dissatisfied with all aspects of life. About 3 out of 4 are satisfied with their lives as a whole, and if we add the women who are satisfied with one aspect of their lives, the proportion rises to above 90 percent.

There is a relationship between their marital status and their satisfaction. As one might anticipate, those whose marriages had been broken by death, divorce, or separation were most likely to report dissatisfaction in this area. The next group were the single women. Nevertheless, over half of the women with broken marriages and two-thirds of those who had remained single reported that they are completely satisfied with their present circumstances.

That so many single women seem satisfied may reflect that some never desire to marry or have children and that others who did intend to marry found that they were able to adjust to a single life without difficulty. Finally, a few may be repressing their true feelings.

TABLE 9.2

Schema of Satisfaction	*Percent*
Satisfied with both areas	72
Satisfied with personal life; dissatisfied with work	12
Satisfied with work; dissatisfied with personal life	7
Dissatisfied with both areas	9
Total	*100*

What about the women whose marriages had been dissolved who reported that they were satisfied with their lives? Here, the explanation may be that they no longer faced the disturbances which had characterized their married lives. They may have found that they enjoyed being in control of their time and energy and able to pursue their own goals without having to take their husbands' wishes into consideration. And some who had children were relieved when their offspring were freed from the tensions which had characterized their homes. These explanations refer to those who were divorced. The widowed group reported a high order of dissatisfaction with their personal lives.

No relation was found to exist between a woman's work pattern and her satisfaction with her present circumstances. The 72 percent who appeared to be satisfied in all regards and the 28 percent who reported some serious dissatisfactions are indistinguishable as far as their attachment to the labor force is concerned. Even more striking is the fact that there was no relationship between a woman's present level of achievement and her satisfaction. Those who had achieved the most in their careers were not more satisfied than those who had achieved the least. Presumably those on a lower achievement level either had had more modest occupational goals or had been willing to revise them downward.

TABLE 9.3

Schema of Satisfaction (in percent)

Role	*satisfied, all aspects*	*dissatisfied, work*	*dissatisfied, personal life*	*dissatisfied, all aspects*
Worker	62	36	80	70
Combination	13	22	0	7
Homemaker	25	42	20	23
Total	*100*	*100*	*100*	*100*

Table 9.3 shows the relationship between the present role of these women and their satisfaction with their life circumstances. Those who reported that they were satisfied with all aspects of their life include women who work full time, part time, or who are at home in about the same proportion as these roles are distributed throughout the group as a whole. In other words, no one role is more likely to include a higher proportion of satisfied women.

The largest group who are dissatisfied with the work area in their lives are the homemakers. And those who are most dissatisfied with their personal lives are most frequently found among the full-time workers. Those who are dissatisfied in general with their circumstances, only a few in number, are not distributed in any significant pattern. It will appear then that broad satisfaction or dissatisfaction is not closely associated with any one role, while dissatisfaction with one's work or personal life is likely to be directly linked to the lack of a job or of marriage.

Whether an individual is satisfied with his life or not often depends on the extent to which his early expectations have been met. We compared the women's earlier anticipations with their present roles and found that, in general, their anticipations had been fulfilled. Those who had expected their careers to take precedence over family were more likely to be full-time workers than those who had not.

We had asked our group whether they felt that their earlier expectations had been met. Table 9.4 sets forth these data. We had usable information for 85 percent of the entire group. Over half reported that all of their expectations had been exceeded or met. If we add to this group those whose expectations were mixed, which means that at least some of their expectations had been met or exceeded, the proportion rises to about two-thirds. Over a third reported that all of their expectations had remained unrealized and this proportion rises to close to half if we add those who were disappointed in certain of their expectations.

Indicative of the replies of those whose expectations had been exceeded were the following. A scientist: "I have had an easier time than I expected in earning a living according to my desires." A Ph.D. in the humanities: "I live a more prominent, useful, and entertaining life than I would have anticipated." A physician wrote: "I have been pleasantly surprised by the measure of mastery and competence and satisfaction I have achieved since I was a depressed, pessimistic, narcissistic individual as a child and adolescent." A bacteriologist reported that she had "never expected to obtain as high a position of responsibility as now have." A guidance counselor: "More than met my expectations. I have held interesting jobs, traveled, met interesting people,

TABLE 9.4

Fulfillment	*Percent*
Expectations exceeded	25
Expectations met	29
Mixed: some met or exceeded, some unrealized	10
Expectations unrealized	36
Total (N = 265)	*100*

have had an extremely intelligent and successful husband, and have three healthy intelligent children. I have an active and satisfactory professional, social, and home life."

Among those who reported that their expectations had been met was a social worker who wrote: "My expectations never soared beyond the walls of reality. Therefore disappointment and frustration have escaped me." A Ph.D. musicologist said: "I am having exactly the kind of career for which I prepared." A government official: "I did what I hoped to do, within biological limitations." Another such official said: "I have largely realized the limited ambitions I had during school years."

Included among those with mixed fulfillment of expectations was a journalist who "expected to be a famous writer at some point and I'm sorry I never made it. But I've enjoyed the years more than I thought post-twenty-year-olds did." An archeologist reported that she had achieved "more work, less home life (than expected), more recognition, a lower standard of living." A medical researcher: "Better than expected in most ways. *But* no Nobel Prize yet—and that childish goal seems more distant now."

Of the slightly more than one-third of the group who indicated that their expectations had been unrealized, only a very few reported that their discontent centered around matters of the family. The major causes of disappointment related to the nature of their work and their lack of achievement, followed by discontent about the conditions of their work or the absence of a career.

Among the few whose unrealized expectations centered around the family area, specifically the lack of children, was a member of the teaching staff of a school of library service: "During college," she wrote, "like most students, I rather anticipated marriage and children. I did not expect to remain in teaching this long." Another was a public health worker: "I expected to have a family which I never did have and consequently this has enabled me to continue working. If I had had children my life would have been very different." Another who was surprised by the way her life had developed reported: "I expected a suburban cottage with children, relatives all over the place, and the *Saturday Evening Post.* I have a city apartment, no children, cats, a professional husband, and the *Times Literary Supplement.*"

An economist reported her work as the cause of disappointment: "All of my work falls short of expectations most of the time." A college instructor in languages said: "I have less respect for the academic profession than I had ten years ago. There is much less time for research and continuing education in my field than I had expected to have."

Lack of achievement was a frequently reported source of disappointment. A journalist: "I had imagined my impact on the world would have been much greater, much faster." An academician specializing in foreign languages: "I have been less successful professionally than I expected, have less time for scholarship."

Some mentioned the lack of a career as a disappointment. A lawyer: "I did not anticipate while at school that I would abandon my profession to stay at home with my children." An historian: "I had expected to combine marriage with career. Therefore that part of my life which is careerless falls short of expectations." Another historian said: "If asked while at graduate school, I would have said that in twelve years I would have been an assistant professor, at least, or a department head at a small college. Instead my active participation in school studies is limited to helping my sixth-grader with projects on Egypt, the Romans, etc."

A few found conditions of their work below their expectations: A medical social worker: "Income-wise: Not as I expected . . . because my husband's interests keep me tied to a place where salaries are low." And an unmarried zoologist: "I have less personal freedom than I had expected."

The relationship between the fulfillment of a woman's expectations and her satisfaction with her work and life is presented in Table 9.5. As we would have expected a significant relationship exists between the two. The more a woman's expectations were met or exceeded, the more likely it is that she is satisfied with her life. The table also shows that even if all or some of her expectations were unrealized, she is not necessarily dissatisfied with the way in which her life has unfolded. This is probably because an individual's early expectations undergo modification as she grows older and is confronted by reality, and new satisfactions supersede early expectations. Others among our group whose expectations had been fully met or even exceeded indicated that they were dissatisfied with part or the whole of their lives. Apparently a minority found that when they

TABLE 9.5

	Fulfillment (in percent)			
Schema of Satisfaction	*exceeded*	*met*	*mixed*	*unrealized*
Satisfied with all aspects	91	78	59	57
Dissatisfied with work	6	9	11	19
Dissatisfied with personal life	3	8	19	5
Dissatisfied with all aspects	0	5	11	19
Total (N = 265)	*100*	*100*	*100*	*100*

fully achieved what they had set out to accomplish, some essential was still missing from their lives.

The foregoing tells us that the anticipations that our women held while still in graduate school about the patterning of their lives, particularly with regard to emphasis on career or marriage, foreshadowed to a marked degree the type of lives that they in fact came to lead.

So far we have considered the relationship of their earlier expectations to their present circumstances. But all people make plans for the future. In addition, however, how these women feel about their present circumstances can be gauged in part by whether they anticipate making significant changes in the future.

Over 40 percent of the women planned to make some future changes involving either more or less activity outside the home. Two-thirds of these are women who are not now working and who look forward to returning to work. Most of the others are older women looking forward to retirement. Of those who do not intend to change, over three-quarters are now working.

However, the simple fact that a large number of women anticipate making changes in the future should not be taken as an indication of dissatisfaction with their present roles. Since, as we have seen, three-quarters of the women are generally satisfied with their present circumstances, it is clear that most of the changes anticipated will be adaptations to current or expected patterning of their lives.

A social worker indicated that "while my children were small I found being a homemaker most satisfying . . . and will work in order to substitute this satisfying experience for the lessening demands and therefore gratifications from child rearing as my children need me less." A journalist looked forward to the same shift. "When children grow older, I will probably return to working a full week and will again give time to volunteer service." The reverse situation is contemplated by a widowed full-time public health worker: "Two years from now when my three children will be finished with college, I can relax on my drive for earning money to accomplish this goal."

Most of the women expect to have more free time as their children grow older and most of them contemplate reentering the labor force or increasing the time that they will devote to their present jobs. A few realize that if their marital circumstances undergo a major change—death or incapacitation of their husbands, for example—they might be forced to make more radical adjustments in their plans. But except for this group the future pattern appears to be largely one of increasing involvement in a job in conjunction with declining responsibilities at home.

Additional education was seen as an important route through which many of our women hope to realize their future plans. Thirty percent indicated explicitly that they had no plans for additional education. About a third planned to take additional or refresher work in their field. The remainder had a variety of educational goals, including completing their Ph.D. or other degrees, entering a new course of studies, such as for teaching accreditation.

Those who had completed all of their course work for their doctorate were most likely to look forward to completing the requirements for the degree. While most of those who had a doctorate did not plan to pursue their formal education any further, 40 percent indicated that they would continue to study primarily in their present field. Of those who had acquired a master's degree, 3 out of 5 indicated that they planned to go back to school.

Many recognized the necessity to stay abreast of the advances in their field and many whose education had been interrupted looked forward to completing their work. Many others saw additional education as a necessary step before reentering the labor force.

These women saw further education as part of their long-term planning. A chemist who had been away from work for fourteen years and who had recently returned to part-time employment wrote: "Would like to study to get up to date in my field." A mother of three looked forward to getting a "Ph.D. in field related to health education. I can't get DPH in Pittsburgh, and I can't leave my children to go elsewhere, so I probably will take my degree in public administration." A government official close to retirement said: "I intend to change my field of work to education as soon as my government pension provides security for more education." An historian: "I hope to teach once my youngest child starts school. I will enroll in Teachers College and get my teacher-certification for high school, since I have 'lost' too many years to attempt college teaching."

In summary, we find that only a small minority of our women were dissatisfied with the way in which their lives had unfolded. The majority had been able to realize their expectations and a significant number reported that their expectations had been exceeded. But even when their expectations had been unrealized, not all our women were dissatisfied. Most of them had found sufficient gratifications from the different sectors of their lives—home, work, and volunteer activities—to be able to absorb their disappointments. On balance, they had had a sufficient range of options to make satisfying lives for themselves.

There is little in our analysis to support the widespread belief that most educated women are trapped in situations which create frustration and disappointment and that it is the rare woman indeed who is able to fulfill her potentiality. The opposite is much closer to the truth.

10

Life Styles

The types of lives people lead and the lessons they transmit to a younger generation are determined by certain basic attitudes and values. This chapter will describe and analyze these attitudes and their effect on the behavior of the women in our group. It will also set forth their attitudes toward the role of adult women in contemporary American society. This focus will serve as a summary of the discrete facets of their lives which have already been previously reviewed.

Since the term "value" is used in many different ways, both in the general and scientific literature, we will indicate what we mean by it. We see an individual's values as the reflection of his basic inclinations and generalized orientations. They are the elements that shape the preference systems he develops to guide him in the formulation of goals and in the exercise of choice. The sequential decisions that an individual makes are not random but are meaningfully related to each other, since his preference system rests upon a limited number of distinct values which give meaning and direction to his life and influence his choices among the alternatives he confronts.

We have identified a variety of "life styles" followed by the women in our group and which rest upon distinctions among basic values. By "life style" we refer to that orientation to self, others, and society, that each individual develops and follows, that is, his value orientation.

This approach confronted the staff with a twofold challenge. First was the identification of different life styles. Second was the evaluation of each individual to determine into which category she was to be placed. The first problem was simplified by our earlier efforts to develop such a category scheme for educated men, which we modified and elaborated in light of our knowledge of the lives of these women.

The second problem was also met simply. In order to determine the appropriate category for every respondent we looked in each questionnaire for the dominant approach underlying the responses to the various questions. In most instances we were able to identify such an approach, although in a few cases the predominant style could be discerned only after probing and reflection. We were able to classify all of the women as belonging to one or another "type." It should be noted that our categories were arrived at empirically and do not reflect any preconceived social or psychological theory.

The first of the four types of life style which we identified describes those women whose underlying attitudes and preferences indicate a striving after autonomy, i.e., women who want to direct themselves rather than direct others or be directed by them. Because of this emphasis on self-direction and self-determination, we have identified these women as the *individualistic* type.

M.P. is an example of the individualistic type. She is currently an associate professor of French at a leading eastern university. "I could never have been merely a wife and mother without making everyone around me nervous and unhappy," she wrote. "Fortunately, I have always wanted to be left alone to devote myself to work, reading, and day-dreaming. My present career is perfect for this combination." Her basic orientation derives from a desire for freedom, to do what *she* wants to do, to be free of obligations growing out of her relations to others. Her own words, "to be left alone," are the key to her personality and life stance.

Another woman, a statistician for the government, said: "My mother wanted me to be independent financially . . . she firmly believed I'd have a happier life. I now believe she is right." Although married with five children, she has worked continuously, and in a few years she and her husband expect to be financially independent and to "retire" to become "our own bosses." With regard to her working she said: "I would not be content to be just a housewife. . . . I must work to express myself—children or no children. The alternative is that I would be a frustrated woman in which case I would be no good to anyone—including myself." Her desire for independence and self-expression is evident throughout her questionnaire.

The second major type describes those women whose major drive is to influence people and events. They may want to dominate others but not necessarily. But they do want to make an impact and have their ideas and values influence others. They have strong drives and motivation. We have designated this group as the *influential* type.

P.Y. is a representative of the influential type. She took her master's degree in student personnel administration with the aim of becoming a dean of women. "There was a dean of women that was a bit of a witch in my college. I think that rather influenced me to be one—different!" From the time she was in college, P.Y. attempted to attain positions in which she could influence and direct others. She has been, consecutively, service club director, regional executive director of a girls' organization, dean of women in a junior college. She knew before her marriage that she wanted to combine a career and marriage, "but the career was definitely to take precedence. I went with two boys (for four years and three years) but did not marry either because of career conflicts and attitudinal differences." Of her husband's career, she said: "Until now it has been largely determined by my career." Her husband was in the Army when they married and he has since started his higher education with her support.

E.P. is another example of the influential type. She made substantial sacrifices to rise to a position where she would be in authority—able to influence and guide, and perhaps control, others. Her greatest pleasure, as she remarked, was to influence young people through ideas. She worked for many years as a teacher to support herself while she pursued her collegiate and graduate studies. She now holds the position of professor of education and coordinator of student teaching. She does outside speaking and writing and she makes $15,000 a year. She identified as the most gratifying aspects of her work, "putting my ideas into operation. Opportunities I have to get to other sections of the country to speak. Most of all, the excitement of the teachers as they find themselves growing."

There are many women whose lives are geared to helping and supporting others. Some find expression for these needs and desires inside their homes, others outside, in their work and volunteer activities. We have designated this type of woman, whose basic orientation is to help and be of service to others as the *supportive* type.

Such a person is A.T. She initially studied literature, but was persuaded by her husband, whom she married in her sophomore year, to shift to a "more scientific career," which she did by majoring in psychology. She had completed one year's graduate work toward her doctorate when she left school because her physicist husband had to move to another city. "I had to decide whether being a full-time mother was more important than my work goals and I decided that nursing each baby for a year plus staying home with the young ones was more important. . . . If a woman wants to create a good marriage it is the labor of many years and much adaptation and rarely can her husband reach pinnacles of erudite or intellectual fulfillment and productivity if she is busy shoving onward and upward too, at the same time." In her lyrical formulation, she saw the most gratifying aspect of homemaking as creating "a safe, warm, free place in a senseless world of poised atomic threat. Here is the Garden of Eden where even serpents have a right to dwell—joy, sorrow, laughter, quarrels, yells—but still deep affectional bonds and a natural sense of belonging to each other and to our little world of garden, friends, children—home."

A.T. has found her satisfaction in making a home for her husband and children. She apparently has felt no deep urge either to put her graduate training to use, as an individualistic type would, nor did she seek a position of power or prestige as an influential type would. She was fully satisfied to find her fulfillment at home.

Others who have a supportive life style are involved in

the world of work. Trained as a social worker, M.C. worked for several years until her children required her presence at home. But she looks forward to returning to work as soon as the children are old enough that they will not require her constant supervision. She described the meaning of being of service to others: "The satisfaction of doing valuable and constructive work which makes a difference in the lives of people, directly and indirectly."

The fourth and last category includes women who direct their time and energy toward improving some part of the community. These women subordinate personal goals to larger aims and goals and devote their talent, their energy, and their means to the cause which they have espoused. Their commitment frequently is to a religious, ideological, or political system. We have called these women the *communal* type.

E.R. was born in Europe and emigrated with her family to the United States in the late 1930s. After completing her graduate work, she taught for several years and then accepted a position with the Catholic Interracial Council in a large eastern city "because of the great need of work in this field." In 1957 she became a nun. Her order lives among less privileged and minority groups, sharing the life of their neighbors. They engage in the same kind of work as do those among whom they live, and they themselves live in small family-size groups. Sister E. works in a voluntary nondenominational hospital. "At the same time, we try to live a life of prayer, and simply to be friends to those around us, those with whom we work, and all those with whom we come in contact."

Sister E's story indicates that her entire life is communally oriented. She lives as a member of a religious group, her work and life is devoted to living according to her faith, and she has turned her back on the accumulation of worldly goods. She is a dedicated person who acts in accordance with her beliefs.

Another example of a communal type is a woman with a strong commitment to political affairs. She is a journalist who switched from newswriting to become a full-time, paid, party worker. "From interest in public affairs *per se* I have shifted to interest in their political implications and their conversion into votes, motivated by my belief in the philosophy of the Democratic Party." She spends at least sixty hours a week in her present job which she considers her "best opportunity to serve the Party." She says, "My interest in politics has converted me from a 9-to-5 employee to a 9-to-midnight devotee."

The foregoing examples illustrate both the strength and weakness of our simplified typology. We did place each of these women in one of our four categories but even their abbreviated biographies indicate that there was overlapping in their orientation. Nevertheless, we believe that we succeeded in identifying the dominant life style in each case and the fourfold schema enabled us to make some significant differentiations.

Table 10.1 shows the percentage distribution of the 311 women according to their principal value orientation. It is noteworthy that slightly over half of the entire group were characterized as individualistic, women who place a high value on self-determination and the exercise of autonomy. Only 10 percent were primarily concerned with directing and influencing other people. And even among this small group there were only a few who were primarily power-oriented and wanted to propel themselves into positions of leadership so that they could control others. Many of those in this group also showed the same qualities of self-determination and desire for autonomy that characterize the individualistic group. The last two groups, which account for almost 2 out of 5, were composed of individuals who wanted to meet the needs and demands of others—members of their immediate family or groups in the community. The supportive type, the conventional prototype of a woman, accounted for less than 1 out of 3!

TABLE 10.1

Value Orientation	*Percent*
Individualistic	52
Influential	10
Supportive	29
Communal	9
Total	*100*

It should be noted that although the women were classified purely according to their attitudes and values and independent of their behavior, their attitudes naturally influenced their actions. We can now review the extent to which these several life styles are related to various behavioral aspects of the lives of these women. Table 10.2 shows the relationship between life style and present role.

We see that those with either an individualistic or influ-

TABLE 10.2

	Value Orientation (in percent)			
Role	*individualistic*	*influential*	*supportive*	*communal*
Worker	70	90	37	64
Combination	11	0	20	14
Homemaker	19	10	43	22
Total	*100*	*100*	*100*	*100*

ential life style are much more likely to work full time than those with a supportive or communal life style. But it is also noteworthy that women with the same life style are pursuing different roles.

Table 10.3 sets forth the relationship between life styles and the satisfactions which the respondents derive from their work in terms of their responses. As one would expect, the dominant values which underlie an individual's life style are related to the gratifications she finds in her work. We see that those with an individualistic life style are most

TABLE 10.3

	Value Orientation (in percent)			
Source of Gratification	*individual-istic*	*influen-tial*	*suppor-tive*	*communal*
Self-realization	29	13	21	15
Personal relations	22	28	20	15
Social significance	24	30	23	39
Conditions of work	15	18	26	24
Nature of the activity	10	11	10	7
Total	*100*	*100*	*100*	*100*

likely to find their principal gratifications from the intrinsic nature of their work. Those with an influential life style reported gratifications from personal relations and from self-realization. Those with a supportive life style singled out, to some degree, the social significance of their work, and those with a communal life style, the interpersonal aspects of their work. The one surprising fact is that a greater proportion of those with a communal life style did not report the social significance of their work as its most gratifying aspect.

Another aspect of the dominant values held by our

group is provided by their opinions and attitudes about the proper role of the educated woman in the contemporary world.

With regard to higher education for women, there was almost unanimity that it is personally and socially desirable for girls, as well as boys, to pursue their education as far as they want and as long as they can profit from it. Moreover, there was substantial agreement that higher education for young women should not be different from that available to young men. Only a very small minority advocated radical changes in college curricula for young women in the direction of home economics and other courses directly related to homemaking and child rearing. A somewhat larger number saw some advantages to shifting the time when women attend college and graduate school. Some thought that it would be wise if women would devote the early years of adulthood to raising their children and then undertake their higher education.

The following excerpts reveal the strong feelings of our group toward optimal educational opportunities for all able women. An educator wrote: "Education—as an enterprise—was designed by man for women. It is basically patterned to their career expectations. Through the years society has imposed different career expectations upon men and upon women even though the I.Q. of each sex runs the gamut from ignorance to genius. The current demand for educated 'manpower' can be satisfied to some extent at least by educated womanpower. . . . If a woman directs her potential into the raising of a family, the potential is still there and can be recalled and updated when she is ready to return to a career."

A librarian who has three children said: "I do not feel

that undergraduate education should be postponed until after one's children are grown. . . . I think my children will be far better and more responsible citizens as a result of the educational opportunities I have had. I only hope they get a chance to grow up and become educated themselves."

An historian argued: "In a society which had long since ceased to provide a woman, whether married or single, any secure position within the family there can be no possibility of excluding women from higher education. . . . From the standpoint of the individual, I think higher education is 'wasted' only if a woman fails to achieve a balance between the activities involved in marriage and the demands of a career."

Another historian argued for women's education on the score that "educated men require educated wives although sometimes they don't realize it soon enough. . . . Women should certainly *not* drop out of college to put a husband through graduate school—the gulf between them may turn out to be all but unbridgeable." Another woman saw a different danger—when "husbands of young women of a certain type . . . expect their wives to go straight on to a Ph.D. *while* having children and keeping up the home front. . . . The effect is to put pressure on the graduate school to relax requirements . . . for the Ph.D., which the husband seems to regard in a sense as a part of her dowry."

A research chemist with a Ph.D. and two children does not even see another side of the argument: "Educated women make better housewives, better volunteer and social workers, and are better able to educate their children. Many men do not perform the jobs for which they were educated either. Many women will eventually use a good measure of their higher education."

Their replies about higher education for women reflected their own convictions that they had profited from the opportunities which they had had; they saw little point in educating women differently from men and they were not disturbed by the fact that for some periods of time women do not use their education in a strictly vocational sense. They recognized that even when they are at home, husband and children and the community at large would profit from their being educated.

Their positive stance towards higher education for women did not blind them to the need for certain reforms. Looking back at her own experiences, one respondent discussed the changes that are needed at graduate school level: "At least when I was at graduate school, the professors were not all encouraging to the female students who planned to marry. Apparently they considered these students a 'lost cause.' I think it is time for professors and employers to re-think their attitudes and to realize that women *can* combine marriage and employment, and that they should not be rejected just because they will not work a forty-hour week. Some ways must be found to arrange more part-time employment for educated women. Otherwise, this country will lose much in the line of intellectual resources."

Many advocated major adjustments in the timing of a course of graduate studies. "It seems to me that there will always be and should be different kinds of women. Those who are not likely to make marriage their principal careers should be allowed to go straight on in graduate work if they are fitted for it. Those who marry early should have a chance to come back later and bring their general education up to date or go on to specialized study if they have the desire and aptitude for it. There is too much work in the world to be done by men alone."

Another wrote: "I think the real issue is when higher education should take place. If women were mature enough after high school perhaps to choose a mate and raise their children, I feel it would be wise for them to do so then. After raising their children to school age they would then pursue their college and graduate training so there is not the long hiatus between obtaining their training and their using this training in the job market."

Others also saw advantages to breaking the educational track between college and graduate school. "I am wondering if it is wise for a woman to go directly from college to graduate work. I think perhaps a few years of work would be wise. If her direction in life is homemaking the woman would likely discover this during the first years after college. If her direction is a career, general experience in the field would be helpful, as would her added maturity. Bearing in mind the fact that many women interrupt careers during childbearing years, it would seem sensible to wait to develop specialized careers until after this interruption, because during the homemaking period it is hard to keep knowledge and skills at a high level."

Another supported the same proposal: "It is difficult in our society for a woman in her early twenties to think single-mindedly about a career. For too many, perhaps, graduate education is a stop-gap until marriage and the raising of a family. Given the already existing strain on graduate faculties in the good graduate and professional schools, the common reluctance of such faculties to take women students seriously is understandable. Even if a woman completes her graduate training, it is likely that this training will have become obsolete or that her interests will have changed before she is in a position to pursue a career. One alternative is for women to think of postponing graduate training until serious concentration on such training is possible. Going back to school is difficult, though if such a course were to be institutionalized in our academic system, it could perhaps be made more feasible for more women."

A clear-sighted respondent linked reforms in education to changes in the world of work. One without the other would not solve the issue, she said. "I think some of the solution lies, first, in continuing to educate women in advanced studies and then, second, awakening the imagination of both universities and employers to the possible applications of their potential. Specifically, universities should expand their adult education programs and permit easy access to courses within their regular graduate and undergraduate faculties on a part-time basis; transfers of credits from one institution to another should be as flexible as possible to suit individual needs; easy access to university libraries, research laboratories, and equipment on a part-time basis at, perhaps, odd hours would be much appreciated by many women whose home schedules do not permit regular outside schedules; a new class of positions known as 'teaching assistants' could be established—the function of such assistants would be to take over some of the professor's teaching load, or even to teach one whole course in the subject matter of her specialty without being connected with the university on a full-time, fully salaried basis. . . . It's hard to estimate how much valuable work, now being left undone, could be accomplished by the available numbers of such women."

The interlacing of the educational issue with the other

aspects of a woman's life is revealed in the following comment. According to this respondent, significant educational reforms would require simultaneous reforms over a wide front. "We need a new attitude towards women. The able ones who can contribute to our society should be enabled to do so. This means well-run day-care centers; equal pay for equal work; making available training through vocational schools for housekeepers who can function well as mother substitutes; dignifying the job of running a home so that those with the skill and temperament to do so can do so with pleasure or can take jobs as housekeepers. We need decent wages for men so that women are not forced to work from economic necessity, leaving their children without proper care. We need to teach our young men that marriage is a partnership and if they marry a career gal they both must cope with domestic responsibilities. Being a wife and mother is wonderful—but it is not enough if one is trained and able. . . . We need to set up special hours of work for professional women—four- to six-hour days, the four-day week, the nine-month year . . . are feasible in many job situations."

With regard to the desirability of higher education for women, our group spoke with one voice. Even on the issue of whether marriage and work should be combined, about which there was considerable difference of opinion, there were substantial areas of agreement. There was unanimity regarding the need and desirability of work for single women and married women without children. It was generally agreed also that it should be made easier for married women who are under pressure to support themselves and their dependents to work. Similarly, there were no real objections to women working once their children were grown. Differences and disagreements were limited to whether married women with young children should work.

Table 10.4 sets forth the relationship between the women's present roles and their attitudes toward the combination of family and work for women in general. The findings are significant. As we might expect those who work full time feel that mothers can work without conflict or that it is a matter for each individual to decide, while those who are homemakers are more likely to believe that mothers with young children should not work. Naturally enough, their opinions reflected the resolutions which they had worked out for themselves.

TABLE 10.4

	Role (in percent)		
Attitude	*worker*	*combination*	*homemaker*
Deny conflict	63	38	39
Think mothers should limit work	22	38	26
Think young children preclude work	15	24	35
Total	*100*	*100*	*100*

Here are a series of view points which cover the range of the opinions expressed about working mothers. One respondent said: "If a woman has prepared for a career and feels inadequate, unfulfilled, and restless because she no longer pursues it, then by all means let her follow and continue in that career." Another commented: "To pursue a career effectively one has to be free of any severe conflict in regard to family and a job; in short, what is most comfortable for a particular woman should guide her, not a particular point of view of what a woman should or should not do." A single woman said: "Of my women friends who are married and have children, those who have the most satisfactory marriages and seem most satisfied with themselves also work. These particular women do not work out of financial necessity. . . . Their husbands do not object, because their wives are better as wives." Another respondent remarked: "For women with a number of children a full-time job means a hard life with serious sacrifices. . . . I have considered this question often and am unsure whether it is or isn't just a 'stunt'."

One wrote: "Although I personally have hesitated, I strongly approve of married women working if their individual circumstances point to it as the right thing to do." Another woman with strong opinions put her views thus: "I undoubtedly would not be working if I had children and feel mothers should not work until children are grown." A single woman presented one of the most extreme positions: "No woman should work while her children are still unmarried and at home unless compelled to do so for the necessities of life (not the luxuries)." But a mother of two wrote: "So much depends on the woman, the job, the husband. If a woman feels a vocation she is only fooling herself if she thinks she can submerge it to diapers and dishwashing."

A married correspondent wrote: "I think that women should realize that there are some years when the children are young during which their career must take second place. But with understanding on the part of all concerned I see absolutely no need to place the issue of career and family on an either/or basis." Finally, a mother of three said: "As to whether married women should work or not—let each make up her own mind. But it would be nice if they would refrain from turning their own personal decision into a categorical imperative."

These different views about the balance between family and work reflected not only the roles which these women pursued, but, even more broadly, their life styles.

Those women with either individualistic or influential life styles feel strongly that it is up to a mother to decide for herself whether or not to work full time even though she had children at home. On the other hand, about 2 out

TABLE 10.5

	Value Orientation (in percent)			
Attitude	*individual-istic*	*influen-tial*	*suppor-tive*	*communal*
Deny conflict	60	79	37	36
Think mothers should limit work	26	7	26	41
Think young children preclude work	14	14	37	23
Total	*100*	*100*	*100*	*100*

of 3 of those with a supportive or communal life style believe that married women with children should stay home or at least adjust their hours of work.

The attitudes and values of the women in our group toward this central issue of family and work are revealed by the range of advice that these women offer the younger generation. One respondent summed up her advice to her daughter: "If possible don't meet the right man until you have packed in plenty of school and travel and men and jobs and living. The most important thing you must do is to meet enough men to find the right one and not settle for anything less along the way. . . . Don't rush to marry for if you marry too young, you will always wonder what you missed." So wrote a social worker, mother of two, married to a physician. A Ph.D. scientist wrote: "I intend to encourage my four daughters to obtain as much education as they can in directions they themselves choose, preferably before marriage." A mathematical statistician said: "I would repeat what my mother did—persuade my daughters to develop their intellectual capacities to the fullest and to be financially independent of anyone." An historian: "If . . . I have intelligent daughters I should, probably uselessly, encourage them to study as long as possible, to have some professional or career training, to return to it ultimately if not continue it along the way. Having only sons, I feel that they will in the long run be happier married to such women."

Many also hold general views about the role of women which carry overtones for guidance of the new generation. A mother of four with a master's degree in English said: "I do not feel that a woman must work professionally or earn money to justify her higher education. She is a better wife, mother, and person, and citizen as a result of her education and this is justification enough." An economist, mother of two, had a clear view about herself and a tolerant view about others: "While I personally enjoy my work and feel it an asset, rather than a burden, I am not a 'great emancipator' and I do not want to be considered the *equal* of a man in all regards. In other words, I am a woman first and foremost and I work outside the home because it makes me a more complete person and I am fortunate in being able to arrange my time accordingly. Nor do I advocate careers for all women."

A Ph.D. social scientist, mother of three, said: "Some women . . . feel there is some disgrace in 'working' when their husbands are able to support them. All women, or almost all women, work, of course. The only question is what kind of work shall they do. At any particular time a woman's (as well as a man's) direction will be affected by her own talents, her opportunities for developing and expressing these within her society and her priorities of responsibility. . . . She should avoid overemphasizing her own importance and thus incidentally save herself from envy of men. She should try to make her best contribution under her own circumstances, not worrying about the things she might have done if only."

A sociologist with diversified work experience wrote: "Women now go to college in droves, many have careers, numbers work after marriage. The significance and meaning of these activities in their lives will be very much influenced by the men they marry, the degree to which the career can be combined with marriage. I can't imagine myself as never having gone to college nor to work—nor would I recommend such an existence for my daughter, but I certainly don't believe higher education is a cure-all for unhappiness or the way to prevent neurosis."

A journalist said: "I frankly feel that too much is currently being made of the alleged 'dissatisfaction' among women with their lot in life. I see it merely as an outgrowth of our relatively overprivileged society—that we have come to feel we are entitled to be happy all of the time. . . . Even a man engaged in the most rewarding, fulfilling type of work would not be able to score 100 percent on this kind of happiness test."

And a geneticist offered the following: "Since I believe

that the world would run most equitably (though not perhaps most harmoniously) were each person given the opportunity for development of individual talents, I think women as people should be educated, have careers, have husbands and children, climb mountains, do embroidery, etc., according to interest and/or ability. . . . It seems unlikely that the half of her genes a daughter receives from her father (and the half of hers she passes on to her sons) will be transferred by residence in her body into the accepted female stereotypes."

The women in our group had different viewpoints about the role of the educated woman today. But we must not overlook the wide area of agreement that underlies their expressed differences in attitudes and values. It should be noted that very few of the group held either that a woman should never work or that she should always work.

There was no real disagreement with the traditional stance that a married woman with young children has a primary obligation to her family. Differences arose as to the alternative ways in which mothers might discharge these responsibilities. Some believe that if mothers have adequate help at home they might work full time or surely part time, while others believe that it is best under most conditions for a mother to remain at home as long as her children are young. There was further disagreement as to the age at which children no longer need full-time supervision from their mothers.

But these differences fade when we recall that these women do not see a conflict between home and work. Most of the group do not find any basic incompatibility between a family and a career, although most of them realized that many women find it difficult to combine the two. They are generally relaxed about this problem since they know that if a woman finds herself unable to cope with the demands of both home and job she will give her primary allegiance to her home and particularly to her children.

The conclusion from this review of their life styles and values is remarkably clear and distinct. Our women are highly self-determined. They want to lead the types of lives that they have discovered best suit their needs, desires, and the pressures under which they live. Expecting a high order of freedom and self-determination for themselves, they adopt the same attitudes and values toward other women.

Society offered our women the opportunity to become well educated. They availed themselves of this opportunity. Next, society offered many of them the further opportunity to marry and to have children and at the same time to continue to work and to pursue a career. Our women welcomed these broadened options and most of them found it possible to derive high orders of satisfaction from both home and work.

II

Work in the Lives of Women

Most women in our society do not pursue their education as did the women we studied. Nevertheless, while the number of women who have graduate degrees will remain a minority for a long time, it increases constantly as more women avail themselves of opportunities to pursue college and graduate education. Our group, therefore, is a vanguard of the growing ranks of highly educated women who will characterize our society in the future, and its experiences have pertinence for those who follow.

In this chapter, we will discuss some of our broader findings and interpretations of the role of work in the lives of women, particularly with respect to occupational choice and career development, and we will compare and contrast the experience of these women with that of educated men. We will review the parallels and differences between educated men and women by considering three stages of their lives: first, the developmental period up to entrance into college; second, young adulthood in college and graduate school; third, their early years after completing their schooling.

By the time a boy enters adolescence, he realizes that in a few years he must begin to work. Society insists that a man work after he has completed his schooling. Moreover, the prevailing social expectation is that he will work throughout the whole of his active years—which means until he reaches retirement age.

Girls also grow up with clear-cut social expectations, but these usually relate to marriage and motherhood, rather than to a career. A young girl in a middle-class family is, however, likely to grow up in a household and a social group in which there is no single model of the adult woman. Her mother may work full time, part time, or not at all. Similarly, the mothers of her relatives and close friends may or may not work. Nevertheless, a young girl growing up in these circumstances senses that it is the man who carries primary responsibility for providing for his family. As she grows older she will begin to appreciate that the status of the family, including the position of her mother in the community, is largely determined by the work that her father does and the income which he earns. This may be only dimly perceived at first, but as girls mature, these basic social realities become clearer.

Important consequences inevitably flow from these perceptions. Girls are under relatively little pressure to concern themselves with the kind of work they would like to do when they grow up. While some are strongly drawn to careers and prepare for them with mounting interest and determination—sometimes exceeding that of their brothers—they are the exceptions rather than the rule.

Despite this fundamental difference in the expectations of girls and boys, both are exposed to the same educational process. They pursue the same curricula and are generally taught in coeducational schools and classes. In fact, there is a good deal of scholastic competition between girls and boys throughout their elementary and secondary schooling. In high school, there is some differentiation in the elective courses which they select, although those bound for college study many of the same subjects. In general, the girls stress the humanities and the social sciences, the boys mathematics and sciences. Part of these differences may reflect differences in aptitude; partly they reflect custom and tradition. But they are related to the process of occupational choice.

These differences continue at the college level; the choice of the humanities and social sciences as college majors by so many girls reflect, on the one hand, their perception that these subjects may be more interesting and useful in attaining a general goal of self-development, and on the other, that they will provide better access to traditional women's fields of employment, such as teaching and social work.

There is no reason to question that girls, like boys, make curriculum choices in terms of deepening awareness of their interests, capacities, and emerging values. However, while some girls select their colleges and curricula in terms of long-range plans of preparation for adult life, the majority are not deeply concerned with their future work or careers. But such a concern is an increasingly prominent element in the planning of young men, not only in their choice of college, but also in their choices after they enter college.

A considerably lower proportion of qualified young women than qualified young men go to college, which is a reflection of the widespread belief that additional education will be less valuable for them than for their brothers. And among those who do go to college, more and more become increasingly concerned with finding husbands. Many young men also become preoccupied with their relations with the other sex, but the typical spread of three years in the age of marriage between men and women implies that more men than women are likely to have finished college before they marry.

The earlier and more intense preoccupation of many young women with the choice of mates means that their planning for their immediate future is much more centered about husbands and families than it is about education and careers. Most young women, especially those from middle- and upper-income families, do not feel under severe pressure to study hard in college or to relate the choices which they confront to alternative occupational roles they might later pursue.

But although most young women are more husband- than career-oriented, not all of them are indifferent students. Many become deeply interested in a field and willingly invest much time and energy in study. They find stimulation in their studies and are genuinely concerned with the pursuit of knowledge without concern about how to put it to use later on. Their educational horizons are also likely to be limited: many can see to the end of college but not beyond. Those who have such a foreshortened view are less likely to take steps to acquire the broad set of tools which they might need if they choose to pursue graduate studies.

However, some young women do have career objectives even in college. They have set their sights on graduate studies: they avoid early marriage as an obstruction to their occupational planning, and they are thoughtful and deliberate about their college courses, weighing their alternatives in light of their future educational and career plans. The approach of this minority to education, work, and life is much closer to that of college men.

The majority of young men, on the other hand, often become more involved in their studies because of the increasingly clear connections which they perceive between their educational opportunities and their emerging occupational choices. Some young men, of course, go through college with short-range educational plans, loosely linked, if at all, to what they want to do after college. These young men often invest much of their energies and emotions in social relations, or they may be more concerned with self-development than vocational planning. There is considerable overlapping, then, between the sexes: some women follow a pattern characteristic of most men, and some men follow the pattern generally pursued by most women.

We have described briefly the similarities and differences between the sexes during the developmental period and young adulthood. The divergence in patterns becomes more marked after they reach maturity. Men can delay marrying without social opprobrium and without concern for their future prospects. But many women who are still single in their late twenties must contend with considerable personal disquietude and social pressure.

Even among those who do marry, the differences in pattern of life followed by men and women are pronounced. The vast majority of women who marry soon become involved in child rearing and running households. After having children, most women, irrespective of desires, interrupt their education or work. If a woman has free time, she may become active in volunteer organizations. Her husband, on the other hand, is focusing most of his energies on getting a start in his career. His life will be affected by his having a wife and children, but his work will be the center of his activities. Not only does his financial future depend on achievement in his occupational pursuits, but the social status of his family will be largely determined by the progress he makes in his career.

The foregoing description, of course, represents the typical. We know that some women, even after marriage and childbirth, keep their ties to the world of work and continue to invest much of their time and energy in their careers. And some young men derive their major satisfaction from their families and are willing to make adjustments in the occupational facet of their lives accordingly.

In outline, and in general, girls from middle-class homes grow up without clear expectations that they will work as adults. During elementary and secondary school they are given much the same type of education as are boys, with the exception that they place more stress on the humanities. In college, they become increasingly preoccupied with the idea of marriage, although some women become deeply involved in their studies. Because of marriage and children, relatively few women go on to graduate school or become heavily involved in careers. They are likely to spend their twenties and thirties primarily in rearing their families. Work has not been central either to their planning for or to their adjustment to adulthood.

This simplified model describes the majority of American middle-class college educated women in the decades following World War II. But the world in which these young women were reared and educated is undergoing rapid changes. The next generation is being prepared for life differently and the ways in which it will respond to the opportunities and constraints it encounters will probably be different. By drawing on what we have learned from our intensive study, we may be able to discover the direction of the changes that will affect an increasingly large proportion of educated women.

The fact that more and more educated women continue to work after they marry and have children is altering the image that young girls have of their future roles. The expectations of whether they will work are also changing. More and more girls are likely to find models for whom work is important. In former generations, a young woman who decided to work was frequently censured by her family and community. A career was acceptable only for a woman who did not marry and have a family. Today, some men believe that a woman's place is in the home, and some women continue to look with skepticism at other women who are work-oriented. And discrimination against women still prevails in varying degrees in the academic and occupational worlds. But to list these constraints suggests how radical a shift has occurred between the past and the present and how much more conducive the environment has become for educated women to pursue careers.

More and more young women grow up expecting that work will play a significant part in their lives. They seek to realize gratifications from work without reducing their desires for complementary gratifications from other facets of their lives. But because of the many differences that prevail in societal attitudes and behavior patterns, many girls grow up with varying degrees of *ambiguity* in their goals. They do not have the support of a single and unequivocal model.

This lack of clarity may result from early childhood experiences: some mothers do not want their daughters to work, others are ambivalent about it. Sometimes their years in school do not help young girls to resolve this question; even women teachers are likely to have differing opinions about the proper role for the educated woman.

Nevertheless, the scope for girls to determine the type of lives they will lead in adulthood has been vastly broadened in comparison with conditions that existed a few generations ago. Today, an increasing number of girls realize that if they pursue higher education they will be able to work even after they have children. No longer are family and career mutually exclusive.

Today, the educated woman's scope for self-determination is broad, but if she marries, the element of dependency will still be present. Her plans often hinge on the plans and needs of her husband and family, which take precedence in her life. And the kind of life the family leads and the income at its disposal still rests primarily on her husband's achievements. At most, if a married woman works, she may make it easier for her family to accomplish certain goals. Only in an exceptional case will her career prove determining. In short, the married woman's status remains a *derived* status.

The single woman's status, however, has changed a great deal. At the same time that the occupational opportunities confronting the educated woman have been substantially enlarged, other changes have been occurring which have resulted in broadening the type of life she can lead if she decides to pursue a career and forego marriage and children. While adult society is still structured around the family, modern urban living provides increasingly broad alternatives for single persons. The educated woman who wants to remain in full control and direction of her life now is able to have a home, a circle of friends, and a sexual life without marriage. A considerable number of highly educated women now feel that the margin for satisfaction without marriage may be as great or greater for them than with marriage in light of the nature of their personalities, their career objectives and goals, and the limited number of intellectually compatible partners that may be available.

Nevertheless, the overwhelming majority of educated women seek to find satisfaction within marriage, in a close and continuing relationship with husband and children. Thus, the educated woman perceives that she must make her plans on a *contingency* basis. When she marries and particularly after she has children, her life will be greatly conditioned by a host of circumstances and conditions over which she will have some maneuverability, but little control. Since they realize this, many young women are loath to make long-range educational and occupational plans. In fact, many move in the opposite direction and select their fields and careers with the expectation that they will have to shift after they marry. They therefore plan for this by seeking to acquire occupational flexibility. This search can mean, for example, that an able woman prepares for elementary or secondary teaching on the assumption that she will be able to get a teaching job in almost any community.

There are a great many factors that determine whether an educated woman is able to work after she has children: the nature of her husband's work, the location of the family's residence, the special needs of her children, the availability of suitable work, and her attitude, and her husband's, toward working mothers. These are some of the contingencies which determine whether an educated woman will find it desirable or even feasible to work after marriage and children.

The fact that a college girl understands that her life in the decades ahead will be largely determined by a man she has not yet met and children she has not had does not enable her to plan soundly for the specific contingencies she will meet in the years ahead. There is no way for her to know how she will feel about many of the situations in which she may later find herself. She cannot know how much of a fight she will be willing to make to counter her husband's possible objections to his wife's working. She cannot estimate her physical strength to cope with a growing household and, at the same time, the many strains of a job. She cannot tell in advance whether she will be able to cope with the pull of a young child who wants her to be at home during the day and her own desire to go to work. These are some of the many contingencies she may face and toward which she cannot judge her reaction in advance.

Imbedded in the concept of contingency is a process of confrontation and response. A woman will learn what she wants and what price she is willing to pay only after she has had an opportunity actually to experience different situations and to try out various approaches. As she acquires understanding and insight about her many different needs and desires and about the extent to which reality may facilitate or hinder her from satisfying them, she will need to experiment with the articulation of the two. But she cannot work this out in advance either, for this articulation is more than an intellectual exercise. It requires continual balancing of her conflicting and complementary needs and desires, and those of her husband, her children, and her employer.

The first radical shift in the lives of most educated women comes when they leave school or work for the responsibilities of marriage and child rearing. Some fifteen to twenty years later when their children are grown, they may again find their circumstances vastly altered and may make another substantial change in their pattern of work and life. Educated women must not only cope with many contingencies, but they must be prepared to shift the basic patterning of their lives as their circumstances shift.

The place of work in the lives of educated women can be considered to be the outcome of these three interacting constellations: ambiguous models of an alternative life style, broadened scope for self-determination and the perpetuation of derived status, changes in life circumstances which require contingency planning. Since each of these constellations is constructed in terms of several elements, the number of possible resolutions is indeed substantial. No category scheme or model can do more than order the major elements.

No matter how powerful the influences that are exerted on educated women, the resolutions they reach will vary according to their basic orientations toward themselves and the outside world. Briefly, their underlying orientations are likely to differ in three fundamental ways.

First, these women are likely to differ with respect to their *time perspective*. Some are likely to gear their decisions to the near future while others have long-term objectives and goals. Inherent in this concept of time perspective are such considerations as the need for continuity in work for high achievement, the alternative ways of articulating education, family, and work, the capacity to project oneself and one's family into the future, and above all to know where one would like to be in the future and how to get there.

Second, they are likely to differ with respect to the *fixity* of the occupational goal. Some are set upon entering upon a particular field and working within it in a quite specific manner in the hope of achieving a known objective. Others, at the other end of the distribution, have an orientation which can be described as highly tentative. They may be more or less interested in working, but they have left themselves room to maneuver. They are not wedded to any particular type of work at any particular time.

The third way in which educated women differ from each other with respect to their approach to work is in their *stance.* Some have an active stance. Propelled by strong interests and values, their approach to the world of work is to find a way of making a place for themselves within it. While many of these women face hurdles all along the line, they conduct an active and continuing search for a resolution that will enable them to continue working and to achieve the important satisfactions that work provides them. In contrast are those with a passive stance who have no strong inclinations toward work but who are willing to respond to circumstances and conditions. If they find themselves with time and energy to spare and job opportunities present themselves, they will work, but if they find that their time and energy is taken up with homemaking and child rearing, they are content to leave the world of work to others.

One cannot fail to be impressed with the broadened options of educated women to pattern lives in which work has an important place. As they avail themselves of these opportunities, their life styles will resemble those of men. But physiological or social realities will continue to keep young women anchored in the two worlds of home and work. However, if conventional hours of work decline, men in turn, may increasingly develop a counterpoise to the imperatives of a career. They may seek and find more of their satisfactions off the job. It is no longer simply that more and more women are following the pattern usually followed by men; men are also beginning to enjoy the broadened options that have become available to many women. The place of work in the lives of women is being radically altered, but this change has its counterpart in the lives of men. We are in the midst of a larger revolution.

12

Policy

In the heyday of liberalism and laissez-faire, it was assumed by both political scientists and economists that the individual holds the key to his own future. If he has drive, direction, and discipline, they contended, he could pull himself up by his own bootstraps and rise to the top of the social and economic ladder. Some social scientists considered that this newly acquired scope for self-development and upward mobility was the result of giving the offspring of the poor access to public education, but others glossed over or ignored the role of social institutions, even the school, in the structuring of a free society.

To hold that what happens to an individual is primarily the result of his own actions is still an important theorem, although today the followers of this nineteenth-century doctrine of extreme individualism are only a small number. A more recent and sophisticated view of the development and utilization of human potential starts from a different premise. It assumes that the models upon which young people pattern their future roles, their educational preparation, their occupational choices, the distribution of energy between their work and the other facets of their lives, all of these critically important decisions and actions, reflect in large measure the families and society into which they were born and reared, the quality and quantity of the educational institutions to which they have access, and the economic and social forces that shape and give content to life in contemporary America.

Although the exceptional person is able to swim against the stream and to construct a successful life for himself markedly different from the pattern followed by his relatives and friends, there is no general or universal process whereby the individual, self-propelled, determines his own course and future against only a few constraints in the social setting. This heroic theory has limited relevance for the contemporary United States.

Since external forces do play major roles in individual development, we will call attention, in this concluding chapter, to the range of policy actions that have suggested themselves on the basis of this study of the life styles of educated women. We believe that these recommendations hold promise of contributing to the more effective development and utilization of the knowledge and skills of the most highly trained sector of the female population. We will consider guidance and counseling, education, the job market, and the community and governmental arena.

With respect to guidance and counseling, the first recommendation emerging from our analysis relates to the desirability of providing more knowledge to parents about the opportunities that are available to their daughters to become well educated, and to make effective use of their education and skill without necessarily foregoing marriage and children. Our study indicates that many women are able to combine meaningful work with marriage and the raising of a family. Consequently, parents who want their daughters' future primary responsibilities to involve homemaking and child rearing can safely encourage them to pursue their education through college and beyond, without seriously jeopardizing their chances of marrying, and thus prepare for a career.

Moreover, parents of the new generation of teenagers should know that their daughters will not experience much discrimination either in pursuing a higher education or in finding suitable employment. While their daughters may encounter some barriers because of their sex, it is unlikely that these obstacles will prove more than a minor hindrance in the pursuit of their plans. Proper guidance therefore requires that parents become more knowledgeable and more objective about the vastly broadened opportunities that are now open to young women both in pursuing their education and in making use of it.

Although these first recommendations are directed toward parents, they have equal validity for all who are in a position to influence the values and goals of girls and young women—their teachers, their counselors, and others in a leadership position with whom they come into contact. Otherwise, a gap may develop between the new opportunities and their utilization by those who can profit from them.

Next, major adjustments are called for on the educational front. Some school systems still steer able girls away from a college preparatory course on the ground that they will be able to do just as well if they take a commercial or general program. Furthermore, those who do follow the academic curriculum are less likely to be encouraged to study mathematics and the physical sciences than are boys. This may reflect differential aptitudes and interests of boys and girls with regard to these subjects, but there is no objective basis for such a high percentage of able girl students to eschew these fields. Of course, another factor that has reenforced this pattern has been the correct perception that, until recently, the barriers to further educational preparation and to employment for women with these competences were substantial. But times have changed. First, the barriers have been radically lowered. Second, total employment opportunities in engineering and the physical sciences have expanded very rapidly. And third, mathematics has assumed increased importance in many of the social sciences—surely for economics, psychology, and sociology.

It is urgently necessary, therefore, that those who are in a position to influence the curriculum choices of young women be alert to these changes and that they incorporate them into educational and occupational counseling.

The challenges to the college authorities with respect to young women are manifold. First, they should attempt to provide educational and occupational guidance to freshman and sophomore students which would alert them to the expanding role that work has come to play in the lives of women. Second, they should attempt to stimulate them to crystallize occupational objectives within larger life plans. Third, they should help these young women to consider course alternatives from the vantage point of advanced studies or future employment. Furthermore, if the guidance and counseling which young college women receive are to be helpful, special stress must be placed upon the development of an awareness of both the opportunities and the difficulties of combining family and career.

Additional institutional reforms are required to enable women to develop their full potentialities. Women in search of college and graduate education have long been handicapped by a shortage of campus housing. In the past, legislators and private donors have shown a preference for expanding facilities available to male students. More campus housing should be made available for women students.

Lack of adequate scholarship and fellowship funds is another barrier. It is frequently more difficult for a young woman to earn part or all of her expenses than it is for a young man. Next, government support for graduate education, which in the past has been weighted in favor of fields that women have generally avoided, should be granted for the humanities and the social sciences as well as for the natural sciences. Finally, it should be recognized that refusal to make scholarship and fellowship funds available to young women on the grounds that they will leave their fields when they marry is no longer justified. Our study showed that women who acquired graduate degrees do not become lost to their fields. While they may interrupt their careers for periods of time, the overwhelming majority continues to have an active relationship to the world of work. However, because of these interruptions certain adjustments will be necessary to enable these young women to stay abreast of developments in their field and to have opportunities to complete their education or continue their careers at a later time. Among the approaches that have been tried are systematic correspondence courses, refresher conferences, special sessions at professional association meetings, and the opening of regular university classes to part-time students.

There are other adjustments which will be required to enable married women to return to school or work, part time or full time. If they have been at home for a considerable period of time, they need educational and occupational guidance. While pioneering efforts to help such prospective returnees have been made, there is a deficiency of these services in the community at large. Few colleges or universities, fewer professional societies, and still fewer conventional counseling and placement agencies have demonstrated an interest in and a capacity to assist these educated women.

Moreover, most educational institutions, as well as most licensing bodies, have shown remarkably little flexibility in adjusting their qualifications for admission, graduation, or professional certification to take into account the increasing maturity and experience that many of these women have acquired since they last attended school or worked. The number of able women who have been denied admission to graduate schools of social work because they lacked certain undergraduate preparation, the number who were refused licenses to teach because they lacked "education credits," and the number of nurses and other types of medical personnel who are not permitted to work in their specialty because their prior experience was disregarded by the licensing board in a different state, has contributed significantly to the waste of potential and skill. While remedial action has been under way for some time, reforms have been too few and too slow. The simple fact is that the basic educational, training, and related institutions in our society are geared to the prototype of a man moving along steadily from one stage to the next except for a possible interruption for military service. But this prototype is no longer valid even for men. Every year a larger number of men in their thirties, forties, and even fifties return to graduate or professional schools to refurbish their knowledge, to broaden their careers, or increasingly, to prepare for radical shifts in their careers. In a few areas—such as graduate education in business—academic institutions have demonstrated some flexibility with regard to student selection, curriculum, and related matters. But in general, most academic institutions remain hidebound and do not make the major modifications required to meet the special needs of adults with interrupted education or careers, among whom women predominate.

Much more needs to be done to facilitate the refurbishing of the knowledge and skills of women who have interrupted their education or careers. In addition to the few colleges and universities which are currently experimenting with new programs, every responsible institution involved in the education of women must evaluate its resources to learn how to assist this large and potentially valuable group of mature women.

In the third major arena, employment, adjustments are also urgently required if educated women are to make fuller use of their education and skills, and if society is to make use of these women in areas where their skills are greatly needed. In many fields of employment there has been a long and persistent bias against the hiring of women, no matter how well qualified. This has been true in varying degrees in such diverse sectors of the economy as business management, engineering, college teaching, and nonprofit administration. World War II marked the watershed between strongly exclusionist policies and more tolerant if still discriminatory attitudes in many of these areas. It is generally agreed that government, particularly the federal government, has provided one of the more hospitable environments for the employment of women in general, and educated women in particular. Nevertheless, the efforts of the present administration to increase the number of women in policy-making positions underscore the relatively small numbers who have succeeded in moving up the executive ladder.

Since most organizations promote heavily from within their own ranks, women will be unable to compete for preferred positions unless they are hired in the first instance for entrance jobs. While many opening jobs which were previously closed to them are now available, many employers continue to avoid hiring women. They are not prejudiced against women; they simply do not want to lose a good employee after a few years. But these employers do not know the new characteristics of women at work today. First, there are a considerable number of educated women who want and are able to have continuous work experience. Second, of the many who drop out, a significant proportion are likely to return after a short interval. Moreover, many women are undecided about whether to remain at work or to withdraw for a period of time from the labor force. Their decision often hinges on whether they feel that they are engaged in important work, whether they see prospects for promotion, and whether their earnings are sufficient to enable them to make arrangements which will facilitate their continuing to work. The arrangements which employers make with their qualified women employees often determine the response of many of them to the counterpulls of the job and home.

More employers today are willing to hire educated

women. But this is only a first step. An immediate second challenge to employers is to change from restricting their assignments of women to a few conventional staff positions to placing them where their skills and competences can best be used. It can be stated unequivocably that at present more employers are willing to hire women than to assign them without reference to their sex.

A third challenge relates to the willingness of employers to open their intramural and extramural training programs to able women employees. With the exception of a few fields where women have long been part of the executive structure, such as in retailing, access to training opportunities has been very limited. Many employers see little point in making expensive investments in their women employees since they do not believe they will remain long enough to justify the cost. Cutting able women off from training opportunities is a sure way to speed their withdrawal from the labor force. The employer, by acting on his doubts and denying women the opportunity for training, helps to assure that they will in fact act in accordance with his beliefs.

Many employers are reluctant to promote even well-qualified women to higher positions. Their rationalizations cover a wide range: women make poor supervisors; many men resent having to report to a woman; in case of stress women are likely to become emotional; in many situations it is difficult to transact important business if a woman is a participant; women are often unable to be absent from home. While there may be an element of fact in each of these attitudes, and while every one of these conditions may operate to reduce the effectiveness of a particular woman in a position of responsibility, this line of argument misses the crucial point.

The issue should be formulated in a different way. Is it desirable to pass over a better educated, more experienced woman with more intelligence and potential in favor of a less qualified man, even if one or another, or even several, of these characteristics may have an adverse effect on her performance? Is it not true that the male competitor may also have some potential disabilities? He may drink; he may be involved with women; he may have reached a point in his life where he does not want to work hard.

Although discrimination against educated women in employment is constantly being reduced, the fact remains that with respect to initial appointment, assignment, training, and promotion, they continue to face many specific barriers. Employers have a responsibility to examine critically their personnel policies as they affect women and move speedily to remove obstacles and barriers that rest on subjective impressions and preferences and that are not substantiated by a hard look at the evidence. They should consider the indirect benefits of a shift in their policies which would give women broadened opportunities to compete for preferred positions in the organization. There is little doubt that such a change in the organizational atmosphere will itself affect the way in which many women think about and act with respect to their work. More and more of them will shift from a short-range job to a long-range interest in a career. And their employers will have greatly strengthened their scarce manpower resources.

In addition to the adjustments which will be required if employers want to utilize the potential of able women, other factors must be taken into consideration. Many able women cannot work full time at their jobs. They do have important responsibilities at home. However, many women with family responsibilities are able and willing to work part time or part of the year. While some employers have made adjustments in working hours, in location, in scheduling of vacations, and in other regards, and are thus able to draw upon a large pool of able women workers, most employers have remained rigid in these areas.

It is easiest to introduce one of these adjustments—part-time work—when the individual is able to carry through his assignment on his own and where there is little necessity for interaction with other members of the organization. Part-time work is particularly appropriate for such positions as college teacher, research worker, editor. But the opportunities for drawing on the rich manpower reserve represented by women who can only work part time have not been fully tapped even in areas which have been characterized by continuing shortages. The senior administrators in many organizations are loath to deviate from the conventional pattern. Often, this is because they believe that part-time women workers loosen discipline and otherwise weaken the dedication of the full-time staff. Over the years, personnel officials have seen substantial advantages to a single set of rules and regulations for the entire work force. But this overlooks the high "hidden" cost of cutting off potentially valuable workers because of the rigidity of the rules.

There is also a need for employers to be more receptive to the educated woman who, having been out of the labor force for some years, is ready to return to work, frequently on a full-time basis. Such women, after a little orientation, are likely to be highly responsible and steady, more so than the younger members of their sex.

Two additional dimensions of the changing employment

scene should be at least briefly noted. The first is the frequent rule against nepotism. Young women tend to marry young men with the same background. Graduate students tend to marry other graduate students working in the same or allied fields. Many of these women look forward to a career in much the same way as do their husbands. But many find that they face hurdles in addition to that of the necessity to devote time and energy to their homes and families. Many colleges and similar institutions still have rules which prohibit the hiring of the members of the same family. Sometimes these prohibitions are broad and apply in every position in the institution; sometimes the limitation is more restricted—husband and wife cannot be appointed to the same department. And in some cases, there is only the interdiction that an individual cannot serve under the direct administrative supervision of a spouse.

However, good personnel practice dictates that the fact that occasional difficulties may arise when a man and wife work in the same department or division should not obscure the benefits that can accrue, especially in a period of continuing shortages of academic persons, from competent husband-wife teams.

Old policies do not fit the new situation. In place of nepotism restrictions, employers should explore the desirability of offering employment on a family basis. More and more, educated men will weigh the offer of new positions in terms of the family's net advantage. Will he *and* his wife gain if they move? If his wife is working, and especially if she has a good job, the answer will often hinge on the prospects of her doing as well or better in the new environment. The farsighted employer of professional and managerial personnel must be increasingly alert to these family aspects of employment if he hopes to attract the best people. He must make an attractive offer to a prospective employee, and must offer suitable employment for the wife.

The growing role that educated women are playing in the world of work and will increasingly play as employers shed their prejudices, the hours of work decline, and increasing numbers of the oncoming generation prepare for a life within which work will have a permanent place, will certainly have an impact on the significance of volunteer activities for women. Some women will continue to engage in volunteer activities, but their numbers will be fewer and they will be more selective.

Volunteer organizations have come more and more under the control and direction of full-time paid professional staff. While there is still a place for the volunteer either as a board member or as a worker, the scope for her participation in many organizations has been substantially reduced. While some women find no difficulty in fitting into this constricted role, many others, especially those with considerable professional education, are loath to limit themselves to money-raising activities or to routine chores. They find little satisfaction in either role.

If they are to retain their corps of workers in the face of the increasing attraction of paid employment, volunteer organizations will have to devote more consideration to the utilization of volunteers in responsible and meaningful work, efficiently scheduled. Volunteer organizations can make a contribution to the preservation of the skills of educated women during the years they are out of the labor market by drawing on this valuable pool for their own ends. But to do this will require major reforms.

Governments also have roles to play in facilitating the development and utilization of the talents of educated women. The broadening of higher educational opportunities for women—including such steps as building additional dormitories for college and graduate students, increasing scholarship and fellowship assistance, designing new curricula for married women who want to continue their education—will require a substantially enlarged investment in higher education. Much of the additional funds will have to come from government—federal, state, and even local. In addition, however, philanthropic agencies must understand and act on the fact that if valuable national potential is to be saved, nongovernmental monies must also be made available for encouraging more able young women to pursue higher education and more older women to return for it.

A further need is to expand counseling and placement services to assist mature women as they are ready to return to school or work. Part of this challenge must be met by the educational institutions, part by government agencies, professional societies, and profit and nonprofit organizations. There is a major gap between the need of many educated women for advice and the number of reliable organizations that are in a position to counsel and guide them.

Remedial public action is also called for to remove the unnecessary hurdles that the established leadership of various professions, working through licensing boards, place in the way of mature women when they seek to reestablish their careers. The various professional societies have an obligation to review their panoply of restrictive policies and procedures in light of the best interest of the public. If professional groups continue to avoid this challenge in the future as they have in the past, it will become the responsibility of the public licensing boards and officials. Their elaborate rules and regulations must be scrutinized and adjusted in order to encourage the return to work of highly educated and qualified women.

Since many married women can return to work only if they have household help, current tax legislation should be revised in order to temper this one more problem. In a one-parent home, child care is presently deductible, as a business expense, up to $900, and a married couple is permitted to deduct up to this amount if its combined annual income does not exceed $6000. These restrictions as to the size of the deduction and the maximum family income reflect both the disinclination of Congress to erode the income tax base and to encourage mothers to seek employment outside the home. But since the principle of allowing deductions for child care has been accepted, it appears that it would be reasonable to raise the amount of the allowable deductions and the ceiling on the size of combined family income to bring both in closer alignment with present levels of family income, costs of household help, and above all, with the changing attitude of American society toward mothers' working.

Apart from tax considerations, many families who could afford full-time or part-time help still find it very difficult to find qualified persons. There may be an opportunity for profit-seeking enterprises which have experience with similar types of labor to formalize this casual labor market by taking responsibility for recruiting, screening, hiring, supervising, and paying household help. The domestics would become employees of the "labor contractors." Such an approach might lead to a larger, more qualified, and more satisfied supply of domestic workers.

There are other ways in which married women with children could be assisted. The present structure of child-care centers under government and nongovernment aegis should be expanded and improved, so that they serve not only low-income families but middle-income families as well. The latent demand for such services is probably considerable. This may be an area where more imaginative financial arrangements involving government, nonprofit organizations, and the consumer might contribute substantially to an unmet social need through partial government subsidy, tax exemption for nonprofit organizations, and primary reliance on the consumer to pay the rest of the cost. It is an area worth exploring.

This brings us to the last recommendation, which relates to the desirability of greater public investment in basic and applied research on the development and utilization of the potential, education, skills, and competences of the female portion of the population. While we favor more research on the development of talent in general, the environment in which girls and young women develop differs from that of men and therefore demands specifically directed attention. As a research area, the socialization process in childhood, adolescence, and young adulthood should therefore have high priority.

The time has come for our society to realize that women have half of the nation's most valuable resource—human talent. But they must be afforded the opportunity to develop it and to utilize it. A democratic society that places barriers in the way of full utilization of the potential of half of its citizenry is violating its commitment to basic traditions of freedom and equality of opportunity, which in turn carries the cost of slowing its progress.

This argues strongly for the removal of barriers inherited from the past that have led to the continuing waste of resources and to the underutilization of skill. The elimination of these barriers will enhance the scope for self-determination for women. And the enlargement of freedom for all members of a democracy is the best assurance for its continuing prosperity and well-being.

APPENDIX

Questionnaire Used in Life Styles Study

► EDUCATION

1 Please list the following information for all schools attended, including Columbia and its affiliates.

Name and Location	*Major*	*Dates attended and degree(s) received*
COLLEGE(S)		
GRADUATE SCHOOL(S)		

2 Where were you born?__________ *(city)* __________ *(state)* When?__________

3 Where did you live during your high school years?__________ *(city)* __________ *(state)*

4 Did you have any educational, occupational, or other goals in mind:

	Yes	*No*	IF SO, WHAT WERE THEY?
While in college?	( )	( )	__________
Upon completing college?	( )	( )	__________
During graduate studies?	( )	( )	__________
Upon completing graduate studies?	( )	( )	__________

5 What made you decide to undertake graduate education? (If you had more than one period of graduate education, answer for each period.) __________

*a. What determined your choice of major in graduate school?*__________

*b. Did you consider studying any other subjects? Yes ( ) No ( ) Why did you reject them?*__________

c. In light of subsequent experience do you believe you made a satisfactory choice? Yes ( ) No ( ) WHY?

6 Did any of the following factors significantly affect your pursuit of graduate education?

	aided	hindered		aided	hindered
Parents' financial resources	( )	( )	*Military service*	( )	( )
Intellectual-cultural atmosphere of home	( )	( )	*Fellowship or scholarship*	( )	( )
Responsibility for parents	( )	( )	*Full or part time employment*	( )	( )
Undergraduate preparation	( )	( )	*Marriage or children*	( )	( )
Extracurricular or social activities	( )	( )	*Other (Please specify)*________	( )	( )

*a. Which of these factors had a pronounced effect? Please explain.*________

____

____

7 Did you engage in part-time or summer employment during college or graduate school? *Yes* ( ) *No* ( ) If so, at what kind of work?________

____

*a. What effect, if any, did this experience have on your later development?*________

____

____

8 If you undertook additional graduate education in your original or in a new field, why did you undertake it and how did it affect your later development?________

____

____

____

____

9 When you made decisions regarding graduate education, were you aware of any problems involved in combining marriage and a career? *Yes* ( ) *No* ( ) Please explain________

____

____

____

____

10 In what way has your formal education contributed to your present activities or way of life?________

____

____

____

____

11 On balance, how do your experiences since leaving school compare with your expectations during your school years?

____

____

____

____

____

▶ PRESENT AND PAST ACTIVITIES

12 At present, in which of the following activities are you engaged and approximately how much time do you devote to each?

	# hours weekly
Salaried employment ______	______
Self-employment ______	______
Consulting, free lance work, independent research, etc. (specify which) ______	______
Volunteer and organizational work ______	______
Education (including study time) ______	______
Other (specify) ______	______

a. *Which of these activities, regardless of the time involved, tends to shape your other pursuits?* ______

13 Employment history: please list all full-time or major part-time employment since college. Work back from most recent employment. Include self-employement or free lance work.

Dates

Dates		
FROM	Employer, Location	*Reason for leaving this job*
TO	*Job title & major duty* *Average # hours per week devoted to job* *Salary:*	*Reason for taking this job*
FROM	Employer, Location	*Reason for leaving this job*
TO	*Job title & major duty* *Average # hours per week devoted to job* *Salary:*	*Reason for taking this job*
FROM	Employer, Location	*Reason for leaving this job*
TO	*Job title & major duty* *Average # hours per week devoted to job* *Salary:*	*Reason for taking this job*
FROM	Employer, Location	*Reason for leaving this job*
TO	*Job title & major duty* *Average # hours per week devoted to job* *Salary:*	*Reason for taking this job*
FROM	Employer, Location	*Reason for leaving this job*
TO	*Job title & major duty* *Average # hours per week devoted to job* *Salary:*	*Reason for taking this job*
FROM	Employer, Location	*Reason for leaving this job*
TO	*Job title & major duty* *Average # hours per week devoted to job* *Salary:*	*Reason for taking this job*

If more space is required, please continue on the additional page at the end of this questionnaire using this general format.

14 If any of your jobs represented a major change in your line of work, why did you make this change?

15 If you have worked or are now working, what do you consider to be the most gratifying aspects of your work?

a. The least gratifying?

b. Under what conditions do you think you might change your field of work?

16 Please list all periods, since college, when you were *not gainfully employed* and indicate the nature of your activities (i.e., study, homemaking, travel, volunteer activities, etc.)

Years FROM	TO	*Type of activity*

IF MORE SPACE IS REQUIRED, PLEASE CONTINUE ON THE ADDITIONAL PAGE AT THE END OF THIS QUESTIONNAIRE.

17 If you have been or are now engaged in homemaking, what do you consider its most gratifying aspects?

a. Its least gratifying?

8 If you have ever participated in any of the following types of activities, please describe below.

TYPE	*Years* FROM-TO	NAME	NATURE OF PARTICIPATION	APPROXIMATE # HOURS
a. Business or professional organizations				
b. Religious or ethical organizations				
c. Civic, political, or social action				
d. School or other youth organizations				
e. Social welfare and charity				
f. Social or cultural				
g. Other				

What were your reasons for participating in these activities? ____________________

9 If you have engaged in volunteer activity, what do you consider its most gratifying aspects? ____________________

a. The least gratifying? ____________________

0 What leisure time activities (such as sports, arts, hobbies, etc.) do you engage in? ____________________

a. Which of them are particularly important to you? ____________________

Why? ____________________

21 What changes do you anticipate in the future which would affect the nature of your activities or work—when and why?

______

______

______

a. Do you contemplate pursuing additional education or training? ______ *Of what sort?* ______

______

______

22 Did you ever consider making a change in your work or activities but decide against it? *Yes* ( ) *No* ( )

a. If so, what changes did you contemplate? ______

______

______

b. What prompted you not to do so? ______

______

______

► PARENTS AND FAMILY

23 Where was your father born? ______ Your mother? ______

24 What was your father's highest level of education?

grade school ______ *college* ______ *Other (specify)* ______

high school ______ *graduate school* ______ ______

b. What was your mother's highest level of education?

grade school ______ *college* ______ *Other (specify)* ______

high school ______ *graduate school* ______ ______

25 What was your father's major occupation? *(describe)* ______

a. Were there any periods during your lifetime when your father was not working? *Yes* ( ) *No* ( )

If so, when and why? ______

______

______

______

26 Did your mother ever work? *Yes* ( ) *No* ( ) *a. If so, what was her occupation?* ______

b. When did she work? *(check more than one if applicable)*

before marriage ______
after marriage, before birth of first child ______
during your lifetime:
before you were 4 years old ______
during your pre school years & kindergarten ______
during your elementary school ______
during your high school ______
during your college ______
other ______

c. What were her reasons for working? ______

______

d. What effect, if any, did her employment status have on your career decisions? ______

______

______

27 If you have brothers or sisters, please list by age, sex and occupation. ______

28 How did your parents' attitudes toward women's education, work, and marriage influence your own attitudes and plans?

29 In what ways did your parents' life circumstances (such as occupation, education, social position, finances, health, divorce, etc.) affect your educational, occupational or other decisions and goals? ______

► PRESENT HOME LIFE

30 What is your present marital status:

single ______
married ______
widowed ______
divorced ______
separated ______

31 For your present *or last* marriage:

(If married more than once, please duplicate this information in the space at the end of the questionnaire.)

Date of marriage ______ Number of children ______ Year each born ______

Did you work after you were married? *Yes* ( ) *No* ( ) If so, give dates ______

Husband's occupation? (specify) ______

Husband's highest level of education (indicate last grade completed) ______

Husband's income level: *(Please check)*

$5,000 or under	( )	$10,001-$12,500	( )
$5,001- $7,500	( )	$12,501-$15,000	( )
$7,501-$10,000	( )	$15,001-$20,000	( )
		over $20,001	( )

32 If you were ever widowed ( ) separated ( ) or divorced ( ) please state date: ______

How did this affect your work and activities outside the home?

33 If you are or were married, how have your decisions about participation in activities or work outside the home been influenced the cost and availability of household assistance, taxes, or similar factors?__________

34 How have your decisions about work, activities, or place of residence been influenced by:

*a. Your husband's career or his attitudes?*__________

*b. Your children's needs?*__________

*c. Your parents or other relatives?*__________

► GENERAL

35 Were there any key persons, books, or events that had a major influence on your decisions about education, work, or otl activities? *Yes* ( ) *No* ( ) If so, who or what were they and what was the nature of their influence?

36 Were there any attractive opportunities for career or other long-range activities which you did not pursue? *Yes* ( ) *No* ( )

Why did you not pursue them?__________

Any regrets?__________

37 Did World War II, the Korean Conflict, or the Cold War affect your education, work, marriage, or life circumstances?

In what way?____________________

38 Please comment on any obstacles encountered or assistance received specifically because you are a woman, either in the course of your education or in your work experience.____________________

39 There is considerable controversy about the value of higher education for women, about careers for women, and about whether married women should work. What is your opinion on these matters with respect to yourself and to women in general?

40 *ADDITIONAL COMMENTS:* Will you please elaborate on or clarify any of your answers if you feel that it would be helpful to us and comment on any other points that you consider important in connection with your own work or life circumstances?

Bibliography

"The American Female," *Harpers,* CCXXV (October 1962), 117–80.

American Women. Report of the President's Commission on the Status of Women. Washington, G.P.O. 1963.

Ashley-Montague, M. F. *The Natural Superiority of Women.* New York, Macmillan, 1953.

Bancroft, Gertrude. *The American Labor Force.* New York, Wiley, 1958.

Beauvois, Simone de. *The Second Sex.* H. M. Parshley, tr. New York, Knopf, 1953.

Berelson, Bernard. *Graduate Education in the United States.* New York, McGraw Hill, 1960.

Bernard, Jessie. *Academic Women.* University Park, Pennsylvania State University Press, 1964.

Brown, Helen Gurley. *Sex and the Single Girl.* New York, Pocketbooks, 1962.

Buehler, Charlotte. *Der Menchliche Lebenslauf als Psychologishes Problem.* Leipzig, Hirzel, 1933.

Caplow, Theodore. *Sociology of Work.* Minneapolis, University of Minnesota Press, 1957.

Cassara, Beverly B., ed. *American Women: The Changing Image.* Boston, Beacon Press, 1962.

Davis, James A. *Great Aspirations.* Vol. I: *Career Decisions and Educational Plans During College.* Chicago, National Opinion Research Center, 1963.

Fairchild, J. E., ed. *Women, Society, and Sex.* New York, Sheriden House, 1952.

Farber, S. and R. Wilson, eds. *The Potential of Women.* New York, McGraw Hill, 1963.

Freud, Sigmund. *Three Contributions to the Theory of Sex.* A. A. Brill, tr. New York, Dutton, 1962.

Furman, Lucile. *The Status of Women in the United States.* Washington, U.S. Department of Labor, 1953.

Ginzberg, Eli. "The Changing Patterns of Women's Work: Some Psychological Correlates," *American Journal of Ortho-Psychiatry*, XXVIII (1958), 313–21.

Gruenberg, Sidonie and H. Krech. *The Many Lives of Modern Woman.* New York, Doubleday, 1952.

Hacker, Helen M. *A Functional Approach to the Gainful Employment of Married Women* (dissertation). New York, Columbia University, 1961.

Hansl, Eva B. "Patterns in Womanpower: A Pilot Study," *Journal of the National Association of Women Deans and Counselors*, XXV, No. 2 (January 1962).

Hartley, Ruth E. "Current Patterns in Sex Roles: Children's Perspectives," *Journal of the National Association of Women Deans and Counselors*, XXV, No. 1 (October 1961), 3.

"An International Survey of Part-Time Employment," *International Labor Review*. Vol. LXXXVIII, Part I, p. 380; Part II, p. 490. Geneva, 1963.

Irish, Lois D. "Needed: Unique Patterns for Educating Women," *College Board Review*, No. 46 (Winter 1962), p. 27 ff.

Jaffe, A. H. "Trends in the Participation of Women in the Working Force," *Monthly Labor Review*, LXXIX (May 1956), 559–65.

Kamiot, Arnold. *Feminine Superiority and Other Myths.* New York, Bookman Associates, 1960.

Klein, Viola. *The Feminine Character: History of an Ideology.* London, K. Paul, Trench, and Tribner, 1964.

—— *Working Wives.* London, Institute of Personnel Management, Occasional Papers #15, 1960.

Komarovsky, Mira. "Cultural Contradictions and Sex Roles," *American Journal of Sociology*, LII (November 1946), 184–89.

—— *Women in the Modern World*. Boston, Little, Brown, 1953.

Lundberg, F. and M. F. Farnham. *Modern Woman: The Lost Sex*. New York, Grosset and Dunlap, 1947.

Matthews, Ester. *Marriage and Career Conflicts in Girls and Young Women* (dissertation). Cambridge, Harvard Graduate School of Education, 1960.

Matthews, Ester and D. V. Tiedeman. "Attitudes Toward Career and Marriage and the Development of Life Styles in Young Women," *Journal of Counseling Psychology*, XI, No. 4 (Winter 1964), 375–84.

Mead, Margaret. *Male and Female*. New York, W. Morrow, 1949.

Mydral, Alva and Viola Klein. *Women's Two Roles: Home and Work*. London, Routledge & Kegan Paul, 1956.

National Manpower Council. *Womanpower*. New York, Columbia University Press, 1957.

—— *Work in the Lives of Married Women*. New York, Columbia University Press, 1957.

National Science Foundation. *Two Years After the College Degree*. Washington, G.P.O., 1963.

Nye, F. Ivan and Lois W. Hoffman, eds. *The Employed Mother in America*. Chicago, Rand McNally, 1963.

Parsons, Talcott. "Age and Sex in the Social Structure of the United States," *American Sociological Review, VII* (October 1942), 604–16.

Rose, Arnold. "The Adequacy of Women's Expectations for Adult Roles," *Social Forces*, XXX (October 1951), 69–77.

Rossi, Alice S. "Equality Between the Sexes: An Immodest Proposal," *Daedelus*, XCIII (Spring 1964), 607.

—— "Women in Science: Why So Few?" *Science*, CXLVIII, No. 3674 (May 28, 1965), 1196–1202.

Schwartz, Jane. *Part-Time Employment*, New York, Alumnae Advisory Center, 1964.

Smuts, Robert. *Women and Work in America.* New York, Columbia University Press, 1959.

Steinmann, Ann, Joseph Levi, and David Fox. "Self Conceptions of College Women Compared With Their Concept of Ideal Women and Men's Ideal Woman," *Journal of Counseling Psychology*, XI, No. 4 (Winter 1964), 370–74.

Super, Donald, John O. Crites, et al. *Vocational Development: A Framework for Research.* New York, Columbia Teachers College, Bureau of Publications, 1957.

Tair, Marjorie. *The Education of Women for Citizenship: Some Practical Questions.* Paris, UNESCO, 1954.

Turner, Ralph. "Some Aspects of Women's Ambitions," *American Journal of Sociology*, LXX, No. 3 (November 1964), 271–85.

Wallin, Paul. "Cultural Contradictions and Sex Roles: A Repeat Study," *American Sociological Review*, XV, No. 2 (April 1950), 288–95.

Wilson, Logan. *The Academic Man.* New York, Octagon Books, 1964.

Wolfbein, Seymour and A. J. Jaffe. "Demographic Factors in Labor Force Growth," *American Sociological Review*, XI (August 1946), 392–96.

The Conservation of Human Resources Project

The Conservation of Human Resources Project was established by General Dwight D. Eisenhower at Columbia University in 1950 to undertake basic research in human resources. It has been supported by grants from corporations, foundations, and government. Dr. Lawrence H. Chamberlain, the vice-president of the university, excercises administrative supervision over the project.

The following bibliography includes the publications of the Conservation of Human Resources Project. It also includes several books by the director and his associates which were published prior to the formal establishment of the project but which are an integral part of the more than two decades of basic research on human resources undertaken by this interdisciplinary group at Columbia University. All books were published by Columbia University Press, except those for which other publishers are indicated.

Bray, Douglas W. *Issues in the Study of Talent.* 1954.

Committee on the Function of Nursing. Eli Ginzberg, chairman. *A Program for the Nursing Profession.* New York, Macmillan, 1948.

Ginsburg, Sol W. *A Psychiatrist's Views on Social Issues.* 1963.

Ginzberg, Eli. *The Development of Human Resources.* New York, McGraw Hill, in press.

—— *Grass on the Slag Heaps: The Story of the Welsh Miners.* New York, Harper, 1942.

—— *Human Resources: The Wealth of a Nation.* New York, Simon and Schuster, 1958.

—— *The Labor Leader.* New York, Macmillan, 1948.

—— *A Pattern for Hospital Care.* 1949.

—— *Report on Manpower Utilization in Israel.* Jerusalem, Prime Minister's Office, 1961.

Ginzberg, Eli and associates. *The Unemployed.* New York, Harper, 1943.

—— *The Ineffective Soldier: Lessons for Management and the Nation.* 1959.

Vol. 1: *The Lost Divisions.* With James K. Anderson, Sol W. Ginsburg, and John L. Herma.

Vol. 2: *Breakdown and Recovery.* With James K. Anderson, Sol W. Ginsburg, John L. Herma, and John B. Miner.

Vol. 3: *Patterns of Performance.* With James K. Anderson, Douglas W. Bray, Sol W. Ginsburg, John L. Herma, William A. Jordan, and Francis J. Ryan.

—— *Life Styles of Educated Women.* 1966.

Ginzberg, Eli, assisted by James K. Anderson, Douglas W. Bray, and Robert W. Smuts. *The Negro Potential.* 1956.

Ginzberg, Eli, James K. Anderson, and John L. Herma. *The Optimistic Tradition and American Youth.* 1962.

Ginzberg, Eli and Ivar E. Berg, with John L. Herma and James K. Anderson. *Democratic Values and the Rights of Management.* 1963.

Ginzberg, Eli and Hyman Berman. *The American Worker in the Twentieth Century: A History Through Autobiographies.* New York, Free Press of Glencoe, 1963.

Ginzberg, Eli and Douglas W. Bray. *The Uneducated.* 1953.

Ginzberg, Eli and Alfred S. Eichner. *The Troublesome Presence: American Democracy and the Negro.* New York, Free Press of Glencoe, 1964.

Ginzberg, Eli, Sol W. Ginsburg, Sidney Axelrad, and John L. Herma. *Occupational Choice: An Approach to a General Theory.* 1951.

Ginzberg, Eli, Sol W. Ginsburg, and John L. Herma. *Psychiatry and Military Manpower Policy: A Reappraisal of the Experience in World War II.* 1953.

Ginzberg, Eli and John L. Herma, with Ivar E. Berg, Carol A. Brown, Alice M. Yohalem, James K. Anderson, and Lois Lipper. *Talent and Performance.* 1964.

Ginzberg, Eli, Dale Hiestand, and Beatrice G. Reubens. *The Pluralistic Economy.* New York, McGraw Hill, 1965.

Ginzberg, Eli and Ewing W. Reilley. *Effecting Change in Large Organizations.* 1957.

Ginzberg, Eli and Peter Rogatz. *Planning for Better Hospital Care.* 1961.

Ginzberg, Eli and Alice M. Yohalem. *Educated American Women: Self-Portraits.* In press.

Ginzberg, Eli, ed. *The Nation's Children.* 1960.

Vol. 1: *The Family and Social Change.*

Vol. 2: *Development and Education.*

Vol. 3: *Problems and Prospects.*

—— *The Negro Challenge to the Business Community.* New York, McGraw Hill, 1964.

—— *Technology and Social Change.* 1964.

—— *Values and Ideals of American Youth.* 1961.

Ginzberg, Eli, chairman. *What Makes an Executive: Report of a Round Table on Executive Potential and Performance.* 1955.

Greenfield, Harry A. *Manpower and the Growth of Producers' Services.* In press.

Hiestand, Dale L. *Economic Growth and Employment Opportunities for Minorities.* 1964.

Kuhn, James W. *Manpower and the Growth of Nuclear Power.* 1966.

Smuts, Robert W. *European Impressions of the American Worker.* 1953.

—— *Women and Work in America.* 1959.

Members of the Conservation of Human Resources Project staff have contributed to the following books of the National Manpower Council at Columbia University, all published by Columbia University Press:

Education and Manpower. Henry David, ed. 1960.
Government and Manpower. 1964.
Improving the Work Skills of the Nation. 1955.
A Policy for Scientific and Professional Manpower. 1953.
A Policy for Skilled Manpower. 1954.
Proceedings of a Conference on the Utilization of Scientific and Professional Manpower. 1954.
Public Policies and Manpower Resources. 1964.
Student Deferment and National Manpower Policy. 1952.
Womanpower. 1957.
Work in the Lives of Married Women. 1958.

Index

Academic positions, 21, 25; nepotism and, 55, 114, 190; employment experience in, 76, 77, 80, 84, 87, 88, 139, 185; achievement levels in, 98, 104, 105; marriage and, 109, 111, 112, 124, 126; values and, 146-47; *see also* Teaching
Academic Woman, The (Bernard), 3
Accommodations, 108-29; *see also* Goals; Gratifications
Accounting, 108
Achievement, 95-107, 154-55, 181, 186-87; gratification and, 135, 139, 140
Achievement levels, *see* Work
Administrative positions, 76, 77, 80, 87; leadership and, 95-96; achievement levels and, 98-99, 102-4, 187
Adolescence, 118; decision-making in, 16, 42, 166-68
Age: employment and, 10, 77, 189; of dependent children, 13, 55, 62-63, 117-18, 126, 129, 158-59, 160, 164; group distribution, 24(*tab*), 25; childbearing and, 25, 51, 60, 112, 171; degrees and, 41-42, 184-85; marriage and, 42, 50, 56, 60, 110, 111, 156, 161-62, 169, 170; options and, 47, 50, 56, 57; income and, 97
Allowances, 33
America, *see* United States of America
American College, The (Sanford), 3
Anthropology, as field, 2, 113
Archaeology, as field, 37
Art, 54, 71; as field, 92, 105, 111
Attitudes, 50, 59-66, 132, 144-50, 155; toward work, 3, 4-5, 9, 10-11, 12, 18, 28, 30-31, 34-38, 45(*tab*), 47-58, 73-94, 108-11, 159-60, 171-78; of parents, 8, 20-21, 29, 33-38, 110; field selection and, 37, 38-41, 167-68; toward volunteer activity, 67-71; achievement and, 96-97, 100; of husbands, 109, 111-16, 118-21, 154, 158, 160, 172, 174, 175; *see also* Values

Baccalaureate degree, 9, 10, 80-81; institution types, 22(*tab*); age and, 24, 41
Bacteriology, field, 137
Barnard College, 22
Behavior, 9, 47, 151
Bernard, Jessie, 3
Biology, 4; as field, 39, 104, 105, 125-26
Birth rate, 11; *see also* Children
Bryn Mawr College, 22
Business, 1, 23, 25, 35, 57; employment in, 75, 76, 77, 79, 80, 129; sex discrimination in, 76, 102, 103, 185; graduate study in, 185

Career patterns, *see* Work
Careers, *see* Fields; Marriage; Work
Catholic Interracial Council, 149
Catholics, 22, 149-50
Chemistry, 75, 142; marriage combined with work in, 85, 92, 110, 114, 125, 127, 154
Children, 17, 25, 57, 73; mother-child relations, 13, 30, 55, 62-66, 85, 117-18, 126, 160; planning for, 28, 34, 51-52, 56, 60, 112, 116-17, 156; work interruptions for rearing, 45, 52, 55, 61-63, 81-82, 83, 89-93, 108, 116-29, 156-60, 170-71, 176, 186; orientation toward, 48, 49, 50, 51, 59, 62-63, 64, 82, 120, 138, 164, 167, 171; gratifications in rearing, 64, 65, 72, 141; volunteer activity and, 67, 68; occupational achievement levels and, 102, 106-7; fathers' aid with, 118-19, 158; work schedules and, 123-28, 158-59; maternal support of, 128-29, 141; taxation and, 193
Choice, *see* Options
Cities, 13, 20, 26, 67, 82-83; income class and, 6-7
Civic activity, *see* Community; Volunteer activity
Civil rights, 68
Classics, as field, 36-37
Clerical positions, 21, 25, 87, 90, 92, 115
Colleges, 7-8, 9, 22(*tab*), 27, 114; undergraduate majors, 38-41, 168; status in, 98; curricula, 153, 181-83, 185, 192; graduate school entrance and, 156, 166, 169-70, 183, 184-85; part-time study arrangements, 157, 183-84; campus housing, 183; *see also* Academic positions
Columbia University, 1, 15, 16, 17, 23, 110, 112; student origins, 20, 22
Communal personality type, 149-50, 151, 152, 161
Community, 4, 42, 92, 167; *see also* Volunteer activity
Commuting, 13, 88, 115, 116, 132
Competition, male, 11, 95-97, 102-6, 114, 120, 121, 163, 168, 187-88; *see also* Discrimination
Conservation of Human Resources Project, 1-2
Contingency, concept of, 174-76
Contraception, 11
Corporate management field, 95
Counseling, 137, 192; goal decisions and, 42-43, 180-83, 184
Crafts, 21, 54, 71
Culture, *see* Society; Values

Daedalus (periodical), 3
Day care, *see* Nursery schools
Decision-making, *see* Options
Degrees, 7, 9-10, 16, 23-24, 142; parents and, 20-21; of husbands, 25; age and, 41-42; continuity of employment and, 79, 80-81; achievement levels and, 100
Democracy, 47, 69, 194-95
Democratic Party, 150
Depression, 9, 11, 37
Development: education and, 28-46, 56-58, 98-101, 106, 142-43, 166-69, 173, 179, 181-83; leisure and, 71-72; work and, 166-78; individualism and, 179-80; research in, 194-95; *see also* Achievement; Goals; Gratifications; Self-realization
Discrimination: socio-economic changes and, 11, 172, 181, 182, 185-91; fields of employment and, 55, 76, 79-80, 95-96, 102, 103-4, 186, 190-91; achievement levels and, 102-6, 187-88
Divorce, 13, 24, 36, 120, 121; difficulty, 50-51; readjustments after, 96, 128; satisfaction and, 134
Doctorate degree, 7, 9, 10, 23-24, 43, 45, 142; of husbands, 25; age and, 41-42; employment continuity and, 81; achievement and, 100; field requirements and, 109; family duties and, 116, 117, 120, 126, 154

Domestic help, 13, 129; income and, 27, 55, 112, 123, 193; child care and, 30, 62, 63, 115, 119, 121-23, 164; education of, 158, 193-94

Economics, field of, 91, 99, 138-39, 182; marriage and, 104, 110, 115, 123, 125, 162
Editing, 55, 189
Education, 7-10, 12, 31-32, 129; group characteristics and, 15, 20-21, 26, 28, 31, 166; as field of work, 23, 38, 75, 76, 77, 79, 88, 126, 127, 139, 143 (*see also* Academic positions; Teaching); husbands and, 25, 26, 109-10, 111-12, 154, 155, 162, 169, 190; development and, 28-46, 56-58, 98-101, 106, 142-43, 166-69, 173, 179, 181-83; childbearing and, 51-52, 62-63, 65, 116-17, 153, 154; volunteer activity and, 53, 67, 68; postmarital, 73, 75, 77, 111-12, 116-17, 120, 126-28, 154-57, 183-85, 192; employment continuity and, 80-81, 84, 162; field selection and length of, 109, 174; satisfaction and, 134, 143, 163, 164; values and, 153-58, 161-62, 173, 180-81; part-time scheduling of, 157, 183; of domestic help, 158, 193-94; policy, 180-85; costs, 183, 192; executive training, 187; *see also* Colleges; Degrees; Graduate study; High school
Elementary school, *see* Grammar school
Employers, 42, 102-6, 187-88; hiring preferences, 55, 79-80, 104, 114, 185-86, 189-91; work schedules and, 125, 155, 188-89
Employment, *see* Work
Engineering, field, 75, 95, 182, 185
English studies, 39, 44, 71, 109
Environment, *see* Family; Society
Europe, 3, 37, 69, 149
Examinations, 43, 112
Executive positions, 21, 25

Family: degrees of involvement, 4, 5, 48, 49, 54, 61-63, 73, 74(*tab*), 81-84, 96, 116, 141-42, 146, 148-49, 151, 164, 171; socio-economic changes and, 6-7, 11-12, 13, 32, 47-58, 153, 172-74, 180; group characteristics and, 20-22, 25, 27, 30, 33-38; influence on fields of interest, 36-37, 40, 108-9, 167, 173; hiring policies and, 55, 114, 190; community participation and, 59-72; gratification sources, 64(*tab*), 71-72, 94, 131-32, 133, 135, 136, 138, 141; location and, 82-83, 115, 139, 174; achievement levels and, 102, 106-7, 154-55; *see also* Marriage
Farming, 6, 20, 21, 35
Fathers, 5, 21, 26, 65; as models, 31; education of girls and, 34, 36
Fellowships, 1, 2, 16, 40; family supplement of, 33; application for, 42; funds for, 183, 192
Fields, 17, 23(*tab*), 181-82; selection, 22, 38-41, 42, 108-9, 156, 167-68, 174, 182; of husband's employment, 55, 113-14, 125, 190; working hours and, 75, 80, 124, 126, 127; function within, 76, 77, 80, 90-91, 187; work continuity within, 79-80, 84, 89-94, 100-1, 106-7, 108, 115, 126, 176, 177, 183; sex discrimination within, 95-96, 102-6, 168, 172, 182, 185-86; reward differences, 98, 106; *see also specific fields*, e.g., Teaching
Financial management, field, 44
Friedan, Betty, 3
Friends, 42, 53; volunteer work and, 67-69; work gratifications in, 86-88
Fulfillment, *see* Self-realization
Full-time work, *see* Work

Genetics, field, 163
Geology, field, 113
Ginzberg, Eli, cited, 2
Goals, 28, 42, 180-81; marriage, 8, 26, 34-35, 169, 171, 173, 174-75; education and, 31, 36-37, 142-43,

Goals (*Continued*)
167-70, 171, 173, 184; specialization, 38-46, 168, 182; career patterns and, 89-94, 106-7, 172-74; modification of, 108-29, 135, 140, 141-43, 175-76, 177; satisfaction of, 136-40, 143, 188; values and, 144, 171-78, 180-81; contingency concept and, 174-76; time perspective and, 176-77; *see also* Achievement; Fields; Graduate study; Options; Self-realization
Government policy, 8, 183, 192-94
Government positions, 65, 143, 146; satisfactions in, 87, 137; sex discrimination in, 102, 103-4, 186; marriage and, 110, 111, 128, 129
Graduate Education for Women: The Radcliffe Ph.D. (Faculty Trustee Committee), 3
Graduate study, 7, 12, 155, 166, 169; group characteristics and, 15, 16, 22, 24, 25, 27; specialization and, 23, 38-46, 156, 182-83; employment continuity and, 79-80, 89-92, 156, 183, 184, 185; length of, 108-10, 111-12; childbearing and, 116, 117, 154, 156-57, 171; marriage termination and, 128, 129; costs, 183; *see also* Doctorate degree; Fields; Master's degree
Grammar school, 10, 12, 171
Grandmothers, 122, 123
Gratifications, 14; in field of specialty, 39, 45, 98, 106; income and, 52, 87, 88, 95, 149-50, 191; in volunteer activity, 53, 67-71, 72, 94, 131, 132, 141, 191; homemaking, 63-66, 68, 72, 94, 131-36; in employment, 73-94, 95-107, 131, 132, 133, 135, 136, 172, 177; in life styles, 130-43, 152; *see also* Achievement; Self-realization
Group characteristics, 15-27; development and, 28-46; gratifications and, 130-43; values and, 144-65

Health, 13, 53, 68
High school: graduation from, 7, 9, 10; goals and, 22-23, 34, 43, 168, 171, 181; teachers in, 42, 127; marriage and, 156
History, 2, 6-11; as field, 43, 117, 129, 139, 143, 154
Home, *see* Family
Home economics, field, 38, 42, 109, 153
Homemaking, *see specific aspects*, i.e., Children; Family; Housekeeping; Husbands; Marriage
Hours, *see* Time allotment
Housekeeping, 11-12, 30-31, 153, 158; domestic help and, 27, 122, 123; single women and, 59, 63; gratifications in, 64(*tab*), 65-66, 68, 72, 132; children and, 119, 121; part-time jobs and, 124
Housing, 183
Humanities, 23, 38, 120, 137, 168, 171; work experience in, 76, 77, 79, 87; study funds, 183
Husbands: income of, 25-26, 27, 55, 83, 97, 112-13, 158, 171, 173; education levels and, 25, 26, 109-10, 111-12, 154, 155, 162, 169, 190; influence of, 42, 91, 109, 118-21, 163, 172, 174-75; family planning and, 51; career considerations of, 54-55, 61, 68, 111-16, 129, 147, 171, 173, 174; status and, 57, 97, 167, 171, 173; homemaking gratifications and, 64, 65, 66; death of, 128-29, 141-42

Immigrants, 31-32
Income, 13, 70, 75, 186; education levels and, 7-8, 10, 35, 36, 44, 183; parental, 21, 33, 45, 47, 167; of husbands, 25-26, 27, 55, 83, 97, 112-13, 158, 171, 173; of single women, 48, 49, 128-29, 141; gratifications and, 52, 87, 88, 95, 149-50, 191; employment expenses and, 55, 112, 113; location and, 56, 139; achievement and, 96-99, 101; childbearing and, 116, 122, 123; equal pay reform, 158; taxation, 193

Individual, the: social forces and, 18, 28, 179-80; education and, 32, 38; options of, 47, 144, 159-60, 164; values of, 145, 160-61
Individualism, 179-80
Individualistic personality type, 145-46, 148, 150, 151-52, 161
Industrialization, 7, 11-12
Influential personality type, 146-48, 150, 151-52, 161
Intelligence, 15, 16, 153; options and, 162, 169
Interests, *see* Attitudes; Fields
Inter-personal relations, *see* Personal relations

Jews, 21, 22
Journalism, 23, 39, 150; work experience in, 75, 76, 77, 79, 80, 85, 87, 90, 103; child-rearing and, 118, 120, 141; satisfactions in, 138, 163

Klein, Viola, 3

Labor, *see* Work
Languages, field, 43, 85, 86, 112, 126, 127, 139
Law, 23, 99, 101; of licensure, 55, 184, 192-93; work experience in, 75, 76, 77, 79, 80, 87, 88, 91; marriage and careers in, 113, 114, 116, 122, 124, 128, 139
Leadership, 95-96
League of Women Voters, 57, 69
Leisure, 54, 71-72, 132, 141
Library science, 23, 43, 95, 138, 153; homemaking and, 65, 110, 119; career continuity in, 75, 76, 77, 79, 86, 87-88; achievement levels in, 99
Licensing, 55, 184, 192-93
Life styles, 144-65; *see also* Options; Values
Living standards, 21, 26, 113
Local government, 8, 192
Location: income and, 6-7, 139; urban, 13, 20, 26, 67, 82-83; rural, 20, 92; career continuity and, 82-83, 84, 115, 125, 174
Lower income class, 7

Marriage: work attitudes and, 3, 7, 10-11, 12-13, 20, 29-30, 33, 34-38, 44-45, 81-82, 93, 159-60, 167, 171-78; education and, 8, 9, 12, 31, 41, 42, 108-10, 111-12, 154-56, 169, 171, 180-81, 183-84, 185, 192; group characteristics and, 17, 24-26, 27, 28, 60; age and, 42, 50, 56, 60, 110, 111, 156, 161-62, 169, 170; decision-making and, 45(*tab*), 48-58, 108-29, 174; community participation and, 67; occupational achievement levels and, 102, 139; field selection and, 108-9, 190; termination of, 128-29, 134-35, 141; satisfaction with, 133-34, 136, 138, 140; values in, 146, 147, 148; *see also* Children; Divorce; Family; Husbands; Single women
Master's degree, 7, 9, 10, 41, 42, 142; employment continuity and, 81, 89, 90, 91, 92
Mathematics, 168, 182
Medicine, 13, 23, 39; motivation to study, 37, 42, 43-44; compatibility with homemaking, 55, 62, 108, 110, 115, 120, 121, 126; employment in, 75, 76, 77, 79, 80, 86-90, 139, 184; achievement levels in, 99, 101; satisfactions in, 137, 138
Men, 1, 2, 20, 131, 163; career patterns of, 4-5, 47, 48, 52, 54-55, 56, 57, 96, 166, 167, 168, 170-71, 178; college degrees and, 9-10, 31, 153, 170, 183, 184-85; hiring discrimination and, 11, 53, 76, 79-80, 95-96, 184-85, 187-88; questionnaire for, 16, 17; achievement levels and, 102-6, 154, 171; *see also* Fathers; Husbands
Menopause, 13
Middle income class, 6-7, 9, 10, 169, 171; domestic help and, 13; parental roles in, 31, 56, 167

Minority groups, achievement levels in, 105
Mores, 3, 4, 56, 68; marriage and, 9, 10, 12, 35, 48, 51, 52, 54, 56, 167, 172
Mothers: mother-child relations, 13, 30, 55, 62-66, 85, 117-18, 126, 160; education of, 21, 26; as models, 29-31, 35-36, 43, 119, 162, 167, 173; grandmothers, 122; *see also* Children; Marriage; Parents
Motivation, *see* Goals; Gratifications
Mt. Holyoke College, 22
Municipal government, 8, 192
Musicology, field, 88, 104, 137
Myrdal, Alva, 3

National Manpower Council, 3
Natural sciences, 23, 39, 62, 168, 182; employment experience in, 75, 76, 77, 79, 80, 87; achievement levels in, 101, 104; satisfactions in, 136-37, 139; study costs, 183
Negroes, 20, 43, 68, 109
Nepotism, 55, 114, 190
Nursery schools, 62, 92, 117, 127, 158; government policy and, 194
Nursing, 11, 38, 55, 95, 131; licensing, 184

Options, 1-14, 15; decision-making process, 16, 27, 28-46, 54, 57-58, 144, 166-68, 174, 176-78, 182-83; marriage-career choice, 45 (*tab*), 155-56, 161-65, 171, 172-74, 180-81, 183; broadening and complexity of, 47-58, 171-78; limitations on, 54-56, 81-82, 83, 108-29, 141-43, 172, 174-75; anticipations and, 83-84, 130, 136-37, 139-40, 143, 167, 171; fulfillment and, 130-43; *see also* Goals
Organizations, 53, 96, 98; *see also* Volunteer activity

Parents: education opportunities and, 8, 20, 26, 31, 32-38, 45, 180-81; education of, 20-21; group characteristics and, 20-22, 28-38; responsibilities toward, 49, 54, 59, 65, 96; *see also* Family; Fathers; Mothers
Parent-Teachers Association (PTA), 69
Part-time work: option of, 13, 52, 55; child care and, 62, 117, 118, 121-24, 126, 127, 164; time allotment for, 74, 124, 125, 158; labor force experience in, 77-78, 89, 92, 105, 142, 155, 188-89; income and, 113
Peer groups, *see* Friends
Personal relations: gratification in, 131, 174; personality types and, 146-51, 152
Philanthropy, 192
Philosophy, 2
Physicians, *see* Medicine
Physics, field, 87, 124
Political organization, 53, 67, 68, 69, 150
Population, 11, 60, 66
Professional schools, 7, 15, 16, 38-41; *see also* Graduate study
Professions, 11, 21, 36, 108-9; of husbands, 25; organization activity, 53, 67, 69-70; licensure in, 55, 184, 192-93; status and, 57; self-employment in, 76, 80; achievement levels and, 101
Proofreading, 87, 92, 99
Protestants, 21, 26
Psychology, 18, 51, 99, 182; child rearing and, 105, 111, 120, 122, 126, 127, 148
Public health, 23, 138, 142-43; employment experience in, 68, 75, 76, 77, 79, 86, 90, 91, 141; achievement levels in, 99, 102-3
Publishing, 103; editing, 55, 189; proofreading, 87, 92, 99

Questionnaire, 1-2, 16-19, 21, 199

Race, 68
Radcliffe College, 22; Institute for Independent Study, 128
Ranching, *see* Farming

Religion, 21-22, 26; single women and, 49, 50; organization activity, 53, 67; employment in field of, 90-91, 98, 149-50
Research: employment experience in, 76, 77, 80, 86, 87, 88, 90, 129, 139, 189; achievement levels in, 98-99; marriage and, 115, 123-28; on human resources, 194-95
Romanticism, 50, 71
Rural areas, 20, 92

Salaries, *see* Income
Sales positions, 21, 25
Sanford, Nevitt, 3
Satisfactions, *see* Gratifications
Schedules, *see* Time allotment
Scholarships, 16, 33, 183, 192
Sciences, 23, 43, 137; *see also* Natural sciences; Social sciences; *and see specific scientific fields*
Secondary schools, *see* High schools
Self-employment, 76, 77, 80, 101, 125
Self-realization: voluntary activity and, 67, 69; leisure and, 71-72; career continuity and, 86, 87, 88, 159-60, 161-63; gratification in, 131, 132, 136-38; values and, 144-65, 169-70; work roles and, 166-78; social forces and, 179-80
Servants, *see* Domestic help
Seven Sister Colleges, 22(*tab*), 112
Sex: social roles and, 1-3, 4, 54, 56-57, 96, 109, 110, 151, 154, 162-65, 171, 172-78; work patterns and, 4-5, 18, 95-96, 158, 167; education levels and, 7-8, 153, 156-57, 158, 166, 169-70; discrimination, 11, 55, 76, 79-80, 95-96, 102-6, 172, 181, 182, 185-91; options and, 47-58, 171; personal relations and, 131; *see also* Men
Siblings, 21, 26, 32
Single women, 24-25, 42, 60, 160; options of, 26, 36, 48, 49-50, 54, 110-11, 158, 173-74; graduate study and, 43, 128; homemaking and, 59, 63, 65, 66, 123; volunteer activity and, 67; career continuity of, 82, 86, 93, 96; satisfactions of, 134, 139; as models, 167; *see also* Divorce; Widowhood
Smith College, 22
Smuts, Robert W., 6
Social sciences, 23, 39, 113, 114, 168, 182; career continuity in, 75, 76, 77, 79, 80, 85, 163
Social work, 23, 53, 95, 184; motivations toward, 36, 42, 86-87, 108-9, 149, 168; employment in, 75, 76, 77, 79, 87-90, 92, 131; achievement levels in, 99; marriage and, 114, 119, 121, 162; child rearing and, 118, 119, 124, 141; satisfactions in, 137, 149
Society: women's roles and, 2-3, 4, 7, 9, 11-12, 35, 54-55, 63, 109, 110, 151, 154, 158, 162-65, 167, 172-78, 194-95; options and, 6, 10-11, 13, 47-58, 171-78; education and, 32, 129, 153, 154, 155-58, 166, 167; individualism and, 179-80
Sociology, field of, 2, 43, 113, 120, 128, 163, 182
South, the, 44, 68
Specialization, *see* Fields
Sport, 54, 71, 72
State government, 8, 192
Statistical science, field of, 42, 84, 146, 162
Status: of parents, 21, 26, 167; education and, 31-32; single women and, 49, 173-74; community obligation and, 56, 68; achievement modes, 56-57, 87, 88, 97, 171, 173-74, 176; influential personality type and, 146-48, 150-51
Suburbs, 13, 20, 67, 82-83
Supportive personality type, 148-49, 151, 152, 161

Talent and Performance (Ginzberg *et al.*), 2
Taxation, 193
Teachers, influence of, 39, 40, 42, 110, 155, 181
Teaching, 8, 11, 38, 44, 138; em-

Teaching (*Continued*)
ployment experience in, 55, 75, 76, 85, 86, 88-92, 131, 139, 142, 143, 168, 184, 185, 189, 190; compatibility with family duties, 61-62, 68, 109, 111-16, 118-21, 123-27, 174; achievement levels in, 98, 104
Time allotment: for volunteer work, 53-54, 66, 67, 70, 73, 150; for childbearing, 60-62, 116-17, 153, 156, 160; for housekeeping, 65-66, 74(*tab*); for work, 74(*tab*), 75, 77-79, 80, 106, 123-28, 132, 135, 155, 164, 178, 188-89, 191; for education, 153-57, 183-84
Time perspective, 176-77
Transportation, 13, 88, 115, 116, 132

United States: Department of State, 103; Department of Interior, 104; Congress, 193
United States of America, 6-11, 20, 26, 150; immigrant education in, 31-32; community participation in, 53, 56; individualism in, 180
Universities, *see* Colleges
Upper income class, 6, 7, 10, 56, 169
Urban areas, *see* Cities

Values, 3, 4, 28, 30, 34-36; options and, 47-58, 129, 144, 171-78; personality type and, 145-53; education and, 153-58, 169-70; time perspective, 176-77; *see also* Attitudes; Society
Vassar College, 22
Volunteer activity, 53-54, 55, 56, 171; gratifications of, 53, 67-71, 72, 94, 131, 132, 141, 191; homemaking and, 59-60, 66-72, 73, 94; community size and, 67, 82; sex discrimination in, 103, 185; values and, 149-50, 154; policy, 191

Wages, *see* Income
WAVES, 44
Wealth, *see* Income
Welfare organizations, *see* Social work
Wellesley College, 22
Widowhood, 128-29, 134-35, 141; *see also* Single women
Womanpower (National Manpower Council), 3
Woman's Two Roles: Home and Work (Myrdal and Klein), 3
Women and Work in America (Smuts), 6
Work, 8, 185-91; attitudes toward, 3, 4-5, 9, 10-11, 12, 18, 28, 30-31, 34-38, 45(*tab*), 47-58, 73-94, 108-11, 159-60, 171-78; career patterns in, 4-5, 76-80, 89-94, 100-1, 106, 141-42, 159-62, 173, 176, 177, 183, 186; labor market, 7, 11, 12, 54, 55, 75-78, 79, 95-96, 101, 108, 156, 168, 174, 185-86; education levels and, 10, 12, 44, 80-81, 101, 154-55, 157, 181-82, 184; parental experience, 21, 29-30, 167; husbands and, 25, 54-55, 61, 68, 82, 91, 111-16, 129, 139; volunteer, 53-54, 66-72, 171, 191; gratifications in, 73-94, 95-107, 131, 132, 133, 135, 136, 172, 177; hours, 74(*tab*), 123-28, 132, 178, 188-89, 191; achievement levels, 95-107, 135, 186-88; self-realization in, 132, 137-39, 140, 145-52, 161-65, 166-78
World War II: roles of women after, 7, 9, 10, 11, 29, 171, 185; graduate study after, 24, 43-44, 90

Young Men's Christian Association (YMCA), 91

Zoology, field, 37, 139